SEMEIA 26

Narrative and Discourse in Structural Exegesis

John 6 & 1 Thessalonians

Editor of This Issue:
Daniel Patte

© 1983
Society of Biblical Literature

SEMEIA 26

Copyright © 1983 by the Society of Biblical Literature

All rights reserved. No part of this work may be reproduced or transmitted in any form or by any means, electronic or mechanical, including photocopying and recording, or by means of any information storage or retrieval system, except as may be expressly permitted by the 1976 Copyright Act or in writing from the publisher. Requests for permission should be addressed in writing to the Rights and Permissions Office, Society of Biblical Literature, 825 Houston Mill Road, Atlanta, GA 30329, USA.

ISSN 0095-571X
ISBN 978-1-58983-589-4

Printed in the United States of America
on acid-free paper

CONTENTS

Contributors to This Issue	iv
Preface	1
It is Written: A Structuralist Analysis of John 6 *John Dominic Crossan*	3
"This is a Hard Saying. Who Can Be Listener to It?": Creating a Reader in John 6 *Gary A. Phillips*	23
"No Need to Have Any One Write"?: A Structural Exegesis of 1 Thessalonians *Elizabeth Struthers Malbon*	57
Method for a Structural Exegesis of Didactic Discourses. Analysis of 1 Thessalonians *Daniel Patte*	85
Works Consulted	131

CONTRIBUTORS TO THIS ISSUE

John Dominic Crossan
    De Paul University
    155 North Harbor Drive
    Chicago, Illinois 60601

Elizabeth Struthers Malbon
    Dept. of Philosophy & Religion
    Virginia Polytechnic Institute
    Blacksburg, Virginia 24061

Daniel Patte
    Box 1704 St. B
    Vanderbilt University
    Nashville, Tennessee 37235

Gary A. Phillips
    College of the Holy Cross
    Worcester, Massachusetts 01610

PREFACE

The four essays in this issue are devoted to a single methodological issue: What are the appropriate methods of structural exegesis for the study of "discourse"?

John 6 was chosen as a first test-case because it is both narrative and discursive. J. D. Crossan approaches this text from his own perspective (inspired, in part, by Derrida's work) and examines the interrelation between narrative and discourse in it. In the process he shows the "illusion of orality" created by the discourse (its questions and pseudo-answers). The results of his analysis are thus hermeneutical: they provide a glimpse at what it means that "It is written."

Crossan thus begins by the text to reach broader conclusions. By contrast, G. Phillips begins by theoretical considerations. What is the role of discoursivization in any text (in discourses as well as in narratives)? This is a dimension of meaning (meaning effect) which is too often neglected in structural exegesis. In order to account for it satisfactorily, one needs to go beyond Greimas's semiotic theory by considering the theoretical proposals of C. S. Peirce, E. Benveniste and other linguists and semioticians. In effect, one needs to consider the *pragmatics*. This theoretical discussion allows Phillips to identify various "discursive dimensions" and their markers. His analysis of John 6 shows how this text functions at the discoursive level.

1 Thessalonians is without ambiguity a "discourse" (and not a narrative). E. Malbon's project is to see what would happen when one applies Lévi-Strauss's method (developed for the study of myth) to such a text. Although this might seem surprising at first, her analysis shows that this method can indeed be applied to this discoursive text, and elucidates its paradigmatic structure. This analysis raises, therefore, all the theoretical questions of the relations among the various structural methods and their applications to narrative and discoursive texts. Narrative and discourse, despite differences, are not as far from each other as could be expected.

By contrast with E. Malbon, D. Patte starts by the theoretical issue: what characterizes discourses as opposed to narratives? This theoretical question is addressed, following Greimas, by considering the function of discourses such as Paul's letters, and thus identifying them as "didactic" discourses. In this, his preoccupation is akin to that of Crossan and of Phillips. Yet, simultaneously, his goal is the development of a method allowing the exegetes to elucidate the "deep" semantic system (the system of convictions) manifested by this text; as such he has similar preoccupations as those of Malbon. Following this theoretical part, Patte presents a method elaborated on this basis. His analysis of 1 Thessalonians is primarily a verification and illustration of this method.

These four essays form therefore a whole in two ways. On the one hand, one finds in them complementary theoretical and methodological proposals. On the other hand, the analyses of the texts complement each other and should be compared for the understanding of these texts they provide.

IT IS WRITTEN:
A STRUCTURALIST ANALYSIS OF JOHN 6

John Dominic Crossan
DePaul University

If it recedes one day, leaving behind its works and signs on the shores of our civilization, the structuralist invasion might become a question for the historian of ideas, or perhaps even an object. But the historian would be deceived if he came to this pass: by the very act of considering the structuralist invasion as an object he would forget its meaning and would forget that what is at stake, first of all, is an adventure of vision, a conversion of the way of putting questions to any object posed before us, to historical objects—his own—in particular. And, unexpectedly among these, the literary object.

Jacques Derrida/1/

Precis
The subject of this article needs two immediate qualifications. First, it concerns only a smaller unit, John 6, within a larger unit, the gospel of John, and thus it must be considered at best a *first probe*, to be corrected by, even if also corrective of any fuller work on the larger text. Second, the subtitle should be read in the light of the epigraph. The essay is "an adventure of vision," an exercise in structuralist imagination rather than the detailed application of a deductive method and the precise application of a metatextual vocabulary. I have tried quite deliberately to keep the metatextual terminology to an absolute minimum and to use or create only what this present text seemed to demand.

What would one see if one took John 6 as a unity and officially omitted any historical questioning of the text? What would happen if one attempted by looking at *how* the text means to see *what* the text means? An historical vision could legitimately explain disjunctions in terms of sources and redactions, of additions appended by an initial author, an intermediate redactor, or even a final editor. But a structuralist vision will want to know, even granting all that is true, how did such an appender add it here rather that there, now rather than earlier or later? The adventure of vision is to see John 6 as a whole and to study how it holds together as such.

I. UNITY

John 6 may be taken as an integrated whole for both external and internal reasons.

A. EXTERNAL INDICES OF UNITY

John 6:1 contains the phrase "*After this Jesus* went to the other side of the Sea of *Galilee*" and John 7:1 repeats most of this with "*After this Jesus* went about in *Galilee*."

B. INTERNAL INDICES OF UNITY

There are three internal indications of unity, in terms of theme, frame, and structure.

(1) *Theme*. The general theme of "bread" appears as early as 6:5 and as late as 6:58 and thus dominates the chapter.

(2) *Frame*. There is a precise inclusion between the handling of the Disciples in 6:1–15 and the Twelve in 6:67–71:

The Disciples (6:1–15)	*The Twelve (6:67–71)*
The Disciples (6:3)	The Twelve (6:67)
Philip (6:5,7)	Simon Peter (6:68)
Andrew (6:8)	Judas (6:71a)
The Disciples (6:12)	The Twelve (6:70,71b)

Granted these general frames, one might also draw attention to (1) Jesus' foreknowledge in 6:6 and again in 6:64,71; and (2) the mention of Simon Peter in 6:8 and 6:68.

(3) *Structure*. There is a general parallel structure within the chapter:
(a) Jesus and Crowds   6:1–15   6:22–59
(b) Jesus and Disciples   6:16–21   6:60–71

The first column of verses is primarily Jesus' deeds for the Crowds or Disciples while the second column is primarily his words to the Crowds or Disciples.

There is thus sufficient indication of unity within John 6 to render valid its study within the overall unity of the gospel of John.

II. TIME

The text is broken up by several temporal indices. These may be distinguished as internal and external ones.

A. INTERNAL INDICES OF TIME

The internal indices differentiate the text into: (1) 6:1–15. The *first day* is specified directly by the following two indices. (2) 6:16–21. The *night* is specified directly by "when evening came" (6:16) and "it was now dark" (6:17). (3) 6:22–71. The *second day* is specified directly by "on the next day" (6:22).

B. EXTERNAL INDICES OF TIME

There is also a single temporal index linking the text with an external situation. This is given directly and explicitly by, "Now the Passover, the feast of the Jews, was at hand" (6:4).

Three points may be noted immediately concerning this phrase. It is displaced, disconnected, and disassociated within its context.

(1) *Displacement*. It is quite common to start a narrative with a temporal and spatial index. The standard opening is: "Once upon a time in a land far away." In the present case the order is spatial (6:1) followed by temporal (6:4). This is exactly the same sequence given in the external indices of inclusion for the text (see IA above), when one compares 6:1,4 with 7:1-2: "After this Jesus went about in Galilee; he would not go about in Judea, because the Jews sought to kill him [*space*]. Now the Jews' feast of Tabernacles was at hand [*time*]."

My present point is not, however, the spatial and temporal sequence but rather the fact that the spatial index is given in 6:1, the story gets underway in 6:2-3, and only then, almost as an interruption, is the temporal index cited in 6:4. One expects its position to be immediately after 6:1 rather than after 6:3.

(2) *Disconnection*. The feast of Passover is said to be "at hand." Thereafter, throughout John 6, one waits in vain for some connection between this statement, vague as it is, and the feast of Passover itself. This is what happens in the three other places where John declares a feast to be "at hand": (a) 2:13 leads into 2:23; (b) 7:2 connects with 7:8,10,11,14,37; and (c) 11:55 continues with 12:1; 13:1,29; 18:28,39; 19:14,31,42. After 6:4, however, there is no further mention of the Passover whose nearness has just been noted.

(3) *Disassociation*. The second half of the sentence in 6:4b, "the feast of the Jews," indicates that (a) the implied readers are "not-Jews" but (b) leaves open whether the implied writer is "Jew" or "not-Jew." (For example: "It was Thanksgiving, a holiday for Americans," is being said to non-Americans by either an American or non-American).

III. SPACE

The text is divided spatially by indices which are more complicated than the temporal ones. These may be designated as general and specific internal indices as well as external ones.

A. GENERAL INTERNAL INDICES OF SPACE

The text is broken up as follows by these indices. It should be noted that the divisions are close to but not identical with the previous temporal divisions.

(1) *6:1-15*. The *first land* is specified directly by "to the other side of the Sea of Galilee" (6:1).

(2) *6:16–24.* The *sea* is specified directly by the repeated mentions of "sea" (6:1,16,17,18,19,22,25).

(3) *6:25–71.* The *second land* is specified directly, first for Jesus and the Disciples by "at the land" (6:21), and then for the Crowds by "got into the boats and went to Capernaum" (6:24). In 6:22 there is a counterpoint to the same phrase in 6:1 ("the other side of the sea").

B. SPECIFIC INTERNAL INDICES OF SPACE

Each of the three spatial contexts has been organized or centered around a specific phenomenon, respectively, a mountain, a boat or boats, and a synagogue.

(1) *6:1–15 (first land: mountain).* The scene opens with Jesus located positively *eis to oros* (6:3). It concludes with Jesus located, again positively, in the same place, *palin eis to oros* (6:15). It is only because of these positive frames that one presumes, negatively, that the central event takes place *not on the mountain*. There is thus a triple sequence of on (6:3), off (6:5–14), and on the mountain (6:15).

(2) *6:16–21 (sea: single boat).* This boat receives a treatment somewhat similar to that of the mountain. There is again a triple sequence of inside (6:16–18), outside (6:19–20), and inside the boat (6:21).

(3) *6:22–24 (sea: multiple boats).* This unit is simpler than the preceding one. It has a double sequence of being without (6:22) and then with boats (6:23–24). But this whole incident both separates absolutely what happens between Jesus and the Disciples in the between-time and between-space of 6:16–21 from what happens to the Crowds on the same sea. They do not experience the combination of both outside-time (the night between the two days) and also outside-space (the sea between the two lands) during which Jesus proclaims to the Disciples his outside-grammar revelation: "I AM" (6:20).

(4) *6:25–71 (second land: synagogue).* Once again this unit is simpler than the initial two sections. There is only a double sequence and even this must be considered implicit and indirect. The dialogue of 6:25–58 concludes with, "This he said in the synagogue" (6:59a). The dialogue which then ensues in 6:60–71 is unspecified with regard to space but one presumes negatively, that it is *not in the synagogue*. Hence, presumably, a double sequence of inside (6:25–59) and outside the synagogue (6:60–71).

C. EXTERNAL INDICES OF SPACE

Those internal indices connect, to some extent, with these external ones.

The first land and its mountain are specified but negatively as being "on the other side of the Sea of Galilee, which is the Sea of Tiberias" (6:1). This also specifies, and positively, the sea between the two lands. But it is the second land and its synagogue which is specified most explicitly and positively. The scene is set in Capernaum (6:17,21,24) and is centered around "the synagogue, as he taught at Capernaum" (6:59b).

IV. NARRATIVE

The terms Narrative and Discourse distinguish between *deeds* and *words* within the text. The normal line between Narrative and Discourse is indicated by the quotation mark. I do not intend any other more profound differentiation at the moment/2/.

A second distinction is that between Actant and Action. Actants are the personae who cause certain effects, or Actions, within the text.

A. NARRATIVE ACTANTS

(1) *6:1–15.* Between the external index of space in 6:1 and the external index of time in 6:4, the three major Narrative Actants are introduced, separately and pointedly.

(a) Jesus is introduced first in 6:1, as if he was crossing the sea by himself ("Jesus went"), although, of course, the Disciples are with him. But the principal Narrative Actant may be appropriately introduced first and alone.

(b) Crowds are introduced in second place in 6:2, and they have "followed him."

(c) Disciples finally appear in 6:3 and they are simply "with" Jesus.

Later, with a deliberateness similar to their introduction in 6:1–3, the three Narrative Actants separate and go their different ways in 6:15–16.

(2) *6:16–21.* Only two Narrative Actants reappear here; the Disciples alone (6:16–18), then Jesus and the Disciples (6:19–21).

(3) *6:22–24.* Although the other two Narrative Actants are mentioned (6:22,24), the Crowds are alone in this unit.

(4) *6:25–59.* The Disciples are *textually* absent, with only Jesus and the Crowds explicitly mentioned. It is clear from 6:60, of course, that the Disciples were actually present throughout 6:25–59.

But there is a strange development between 6:25–40 and 6:41–59. Prior to 6:25–40 the Crowds have been frequently identified with various terms (6:2,5,10a,10b,14,22,24). That is, four times in 6:1–15 and twice in 6:22–24. Now, suddenly, they become nameless. Throughout the fairly long section in 6:25–40 they are identified only indirectly, remaining hidden behind such words as "they" or "them." But, again suddenly, they are termed "the Jews" in 6:41 and 6:52 and it is "the Jews" who speak with Jesus throughout 6:41–59. The Crowds of 6:1–40 become "the Jews" of 6:41–59.

(5) *6:60–71.* Once again only two Narrative Actants are textually present, but now it is Jesus and the disciples.

But a similar strange development takes place between 6:60–66 and

6:67-71 as previously between 6:1-40 and 6:41-59. In 6:60-66 the Disciples are named three times (6:60,61,66). Then in 6:67-71 there appears a group not heretofore either distinguished or named. And as with the Disciples in 6:60-66, so now this new group, the Twelve, are named three times once they appear (6:67,70,71).

B. NARRATIVE ACTIONS

There are two main Narrative Actions to be considered in the text: Moving and Feeding.

(1) *Narrative Moving*

In discussing Space and Time, the phenomenon of Moving was already evident. But here I wish to distinguish between Moving in terms of Space and Moving in terms of Narrative Actants.

(a) Narrative Moving and Space

In terms of Space the Moving is rather homogeneous. First, Jesus explicitly (6:1), the Disciples implicitly (6:3), and the Crowds explicitly (6:2,5), "went to the other side of the Sea of Galilee" (6:1). So also, again with Jesus and the Disciples in first place (6:17,21), and the Crowds in second place (6:24), there is a recrossing of the sea to Capernaum.

(b) Narrative Moving and Narrative Actants

But Moving is much more significant not just in terms of who is Moving to where but in terms of who is Moving to which other Narrative Actant.

Jesus and the Disciples

Coming. Jesus comes to the Disciples but the Disciples do not come to Jesus. Thus, Jesus comes to the Disciples in 6:16-21 and this advent is emphasized by the rather awkward comment in 6:17b. After having noted that the Disciples had embarked, it is then said that Jesus had not arrived. "When evening came, his disciples went down to the sea, got into a boat, and started across the sea to Capernaum. It was now dark, and Jesus had not yet come to them" (6:16-17). It should be noted that when Jesus comes to the Disciples in 6:21 they are immediately where they want to be. The Disciples, on the other hand, never come to Jesus; they are always simply there (6:3). Compare, in contrast, Mark 6:35 with John 6:5.

Going. Jesus leaves the Disciples in 6:15. Although the primary withdrawal here is from the Crowds, the terminal presence of Jesus on the mountain alone (6:15) reflects back on the initial one on the mountain with his disciples (6:3). So also do the Disciples leave Jesus in 6:16 (compare, in contrast, Mark 6:45), and (some of) the Disciples leave him in 6:66.

Jesus and the Crowds

Coming. Jesus never comes to the Crowds. It is twice stressed, most emphatically, that they come after him. They move after him, first in

6:2 ("a multitude followed him") and 6:5 ("a multitude was coming to him"), and again later in 6:22-25 ("seeking" in 6:24, "found" in 6:25). Thus, once on each day and once on each land, the Crowds move after Jesus. Compare, for contrast, Mark 6:33-34 with John 6:2,5, and note that the Crowds precede Jesus in Mark so that he comes to them.

Going. Jesus, of course, leaves the Crowds in 6:15. It would also seem that he is leaving them, textually, in 6:59. But nowhere in the text are the Crowds explicitly described as moving away from Jesus. In summary: Jesus never comes to the Crowds but they always come to him; Jesus comes to the Disciples and they never come to him; Jesus leaves them both but the Disciples and not the Crowds leave him.

(2) *Narrative Feeding*

The Narrative Action of Feeding in 6:1-15 is totally dominated by Jesus. In terms of Action, he himself distributes the food in 6:11, in contrast, for example, with Mark 6:41 where the Disciples do this.

(3) *Narrative Moving and Narrative Feeding*

The twin Narrative Actions are closely linked together in that the Crowds come to Jesus, the Feeding ensues, then Jesus and the Disciples leave, and the Crowds follow. Thus the feeding is at the center of the Moving and the Moving is to and from the Feeding.

V. DISCOURSE

The simplest reading of the text reveals how the predominance of Narrative in 6:1-21 gives way to the predominance of Discourse in 6:22-71. But before turning attention to that situation, it will be useful to study the interaction of Narrative and Discourse in 6:1-24.

A. NARRATIVE AND DISCOURSE

(1) *6:1-15.* In this unit there is a section of Discourse (6:5-10) framed by two Narrative sections (6:1-4,11-15). The Narrative is quite conceivable by itself, as if one read from 6:1-4 into 6:11-15. But the interaction of Narrative and Discourse in this small unit of 6:1-15 effects certain very significant results.

(a) The Discourse in 6:5 stresses, just as did the Narrative in 6:11, the complete dominance of Jesus over this entire event. Compare, in contrast, Mark 6:35, where the Disciples initiate the Discourse.

(b) The Discourse here establishes the pattern of (i) a dialogue composed of (ii) questions which (iii) are not really answered. This will be much more important in 6:25-71.

(c) The predominance of Narrative over Discourse in 6:1-15 prepares the way for the opposite situation in 6:25-71.

(d) In 6:5-10 the three Narrative Actants become Discourse Actants, that is, they talk about themselves. Thus in 6:5 Jesus asks the Disciples about the Crowds: "How are *we* to buy bread, so that *these* people may eat?" This will also be of future importance.

(e) The Discourse between Jesus and the Disciples in 6:5-10 contains a single Discourse Actant who, unlike the preceding case, is never a Narrative Actant. Yet this Discourse Actant is the necessary basis for the continuance of both Narrative and Discourse. In 6:8 Andrew says, "There is a lad here who has five barley loaves and two fish." When one notices that this Discourse Actant is absent in Mark 6:38, one might well wonder if it has a function here in John. At the very least, it is a first alert to the possibility of Discourse Actants who are not Narrative Actants, who appear only in the Discourse and yet on whom the whole Narrative and Discourse may depend.

(2) *6:16-21.* In this unit there is again Discourse (unanswered dialogue) in 6:20 within Narrative frames in 6:16-19 and 6:21. Once again the Narrative is conceivable without the Discourse and once again Narrative Actants cross the quotation marks to become Discourse Actants. Jesus talks about himself to the Disciples and about them to themselves.

But now, in contrast to 6:1-15, the Discourse is extremely important. In Mark 6:49-50 the frightened disciples "thought it was a ghost, and cried out; for they all saw him and were terrified." In such a situation the phrase may well be translated by the reassuring, "It is I." But not so in John where there is not mention of non-recognition. There is, of course, fear which is the proper response of numinous awe. In such a context, then, the phrase must be given full transcendental value. Given absolutely, without any qualification or addition, it breaks the rules of grammar and must be taken precisely as such a breach. Jesus says: I AM.

B. NARRATIVE ACTANTS AND DISCOURSE ACTANTS

A distinction was noted above between Narrative-Discourse Actants and pure Discourse Actants, between Actants appearing in both Narrative and Discourse and those appearing only in Discourse. These latter now require further study.

(1) *The Presence of Discourse Actants*

The following are the major Discourse Actants to be noted in 6:25-71.

(a) Jesus introduces God under various titles. The first mention is of "God the Father" (6:27) and thereafter one finds "God" (6:29,33,46), "my Father" (6:32,40), "the Father" (6:37,44,45,46 twice,57,65), "the living Father" (6:57), and "Him Who Sent Me" (6:38,39). The Crowds refer to God, once as "God" (6:28) and once as "He" (6:31). The Disciples do not mention any Discourse Actant but the Twelve mention God in addressing Jesus as "the Holy One of God" (6:69).

(b) Jesus speaks of the "Son of Man," once to the Crowds, once to "the Jews," and once to the Disciples (6:27,53,62). He also refers to "Him

Whom He Has Sent" (6:29), and to "the Son" (6:40). There are no such references for either Crowds or Disciples, but the Twelve address Jesus as "the Holy One of God" (6:69).

(c) Jesus refers to "Moses" (6:32), "the prophets" (6:45), and "your fathers" (6:49). The Crowds also refer to "our fathers" (6:31). The Crowds refer to the parents of Jesus: "Jesus, the son of Joseph, whose father and mother we know" (6:42).

(d) Finally, and most importantly, there is a group designated repeatedly by Jesus, and nobody else, with such expressions as (i) "he who . . ." (6:35,47), or (ii) "all who . . ." (6:37,39,40,45), or (iii) "anyone who . . ." (6:50,51), or "no one . . . unless . . ." (6:44,65).

(2) *The Dominance of Discourse Actants*

There are two facets to this domination. First, once certain Discourse Actants appear they dominate not only the succeeding Discourse but even the preceding Narrative as well. These Discourse Actants *absorb* and *consume* (the verbs are not innocently chosen) the Narrative Actants themselves. Second, the apparent exception to that generality is Jesus. In this case all the mediator Discourse Actants are absorbed along with the Narrative Actant Jesus into the Narrative-Discourse Actant, the "I" of Jesus. Here it is this Narrative-Discourse Actant which continues to dominate the text and which *absorbs* and *consumes* the Narrative Actant Jesus himself.

(a) *God.* The domination of this Discourse Actant over the entire text, both Narrative and Discourse, will be discussed below under C.

(b) *Jesus.* After the supreme and unqualified revelation of "I AM" in 6:20, it is not very surprising that the "I" of Jesus should dominate the Discourse. This is effected in two ways. First, of course, only Jesus uses "I" within the Discourse. The Disciples/Twelve (6:68-69) and the Crowds (6:28,30,34,52) use "we." Second, and more importantly, all other mediating Discourse Actants are absorbed into this "I" of Jesus. Thus anything said of the Discourse Actants such as "Son of Man," or "Son," or "Him Who He Has Sent" is repeated also in terms of the "I" of Jesus, with one very important exception:

Son of Man. In 6:27 it is the "Son of Man" who "will give" them "the food which endures for eternal life." But in 6:50-51, "I shall give" (51) this bread "that a man may eat of it and not die" (50). Again, what is said of the "Son of Man" in 6:53 is repeated of the "I" of Jesus in 6:54: "unless you eat the flesh of the Son of man and drink his blood, you have no life in you; he who eats my flesh and drinks my blood has eternal life."

Son. In 6:40 it is a question of "every one who sees the Son and believes in him . . ." but in 6:36, "you have seen me and yet you do not believe."

The Sent One. In 6:29 Jesus refers to "him whom he has sent" but in 6:38 it is a case of "him who sent me."

Finally, there is the statement in 6:62, "What if you were to see the Son of Man ascending where he was before?" Nowhere in John 6 is there any mention of the "I" of Jesus ascending to heaven. This leaves an unfulfilled expectation reminding us that John 6 is part of a wider unity and 6:62 will be repeated in terms of the "I" of Jesus only much later in 20:17: "I am ascending to my Father."

In summary, then, the Narrative Actant Jesus and also the mediator Discourse Actants such as "Son of Man," "Son," and "Sent One," are absorbed into and consumed by the Narrative-Discourse Actant, the "I" of Jesus.

(c) *The Crowds and "The Jews."* One could imagine three types of pronominal interaction within Discourse:

"*I-You*": speaker and hearer interact as reciprocating "I" and "You" in their mutual Discourse.

"*I-He*": speaker interacts reciprocally with another than the hearer in his own Discourse.

"*You-He*": speaker has the hearer ("you") and another ("he") interact reciprocally in his own Discourse.

In the light of these possibilities, there is a very strange change between Jesus' dialogue with the unspecified Crowds in 6:25-34 and the specified "Jews" in 6:35-38.

In dialogue with the Crowds (i) there is not a single instance of "I-He" Discourse but (ii) "I-You" (6:26,30,32a,34) and (iii) "You-He" (6:27,29,32 twice) are about evenly distributed. Note, for example, how 6:26 ("I-You") shifts to 6:27 ("You-He"), or again how 6:32a ("I-You") moves to 6:32b ("You-He").

But in dialogue with "the Jews" all this changes completely. (i) Now "I-He" dominates completely (6:35b,37,38,39,40,44,45b,54,56,57) so that (ii) only three uses of "I-You" (6:36,47a,53a) and (iii) only one use of "You-He" appear (6:53b). Note, for example, how 6:53-54 move from "I-You" (53a) to "You-He" (53b) to "I-He" (54).

This means, in summary, that the "You" of the Crowds/"Jews" disappears almost completely. It is displaced and absorbed by the reiterated mentions of the new Discourse Actant, "He who . . ." (see B.1.d above).

(d) *The Disciples.* There is a rather similar development in the case of the Disciples. Although there is no such sheer numerical predominance of "I-He" as previously in 6:25-59 for the Crowds and "the Jews," it is clear, in 6:60-66, that (i) "I-He" gets the last word in 6:65b ("no one can come to me unless it is granted him by the Father") despite about even usage of (ii) "I-You" (6:63,65a) and (iii) "You-He" (6:62).

Like the Crowds and "the Jews," the departing Disciples lose their "You" into "He who . . ." ("no one . . . unless . . .").

(e) *The Twelve.* In 6:67-71 the dialogue is exclusively "I-You" with nothing of either "I-He" or "You-He." But I am not inclined to read this as a terminal exaltation of "I-You" over the other forms of dialogue in John 6. First, there is the evident and supreme approbation contained in the reiterated "I-He" expressions noted above. Second, there is the fact that 6:67-71 is very deliberately open to the future of the gospel as a whole. This derives not only from the instability effected by the positive and negative poles of "*Simon* Peter" in 6:68 and "Judas the son of *Simon* Iscariot" in 6:71, but also from the fact that, at this stage, we do not know what it might mean "to betray him."

In conclusion, then, the Narrative-Discourse Actant, the "I" of Jesus has taken over the Discourse completely but the most important recipient of this dialogue is "I-He" so that it is the "He-who . . ." that is the counterpart of the "I" of Jesus.

C. NARRATIVE ACTIONS AND DISCOURSE ACTIONS

A very similar process takes place between Narrative and Discourse Actions as that just seen for Narrative and Discourse Actants.

(1) *The Presence of Discourse Actions*

There were two Narrative Actions considered earlier: Moving and Feeding. In the Discourse two new Discourse Actions are introduced. But these are not new in the way that the added Discourse Actants (God, Son of Man, etc.) were new, that is, not previously mentioned in the Narrative. They are new because they are the transcendental equivalents of the earlier Narrative Actions of Moving and Feeding. The Discourse Actions are Narrative Actions of Moving and Feeding. The Discourse Actions are transcendental Moving and the transcendental Feeding. But, as with the Discourse Actants, once these Discourse Actions are introduced they dominate both the Narrative and the Discourse by absorbing and consuming the Narrative Actions within themselves.

(a) Narrative Moving and Discourse Moving

In discussing the Narrative Action of Moving above, I distinguished between Moving in Space and Moving between Actants. So also here with Discourse Moving.

Discourse Moving in Space

Narrative Moving in Space was rather uniform: Jesus and the Disciples (6:1-3), and then the Crowds (6:2,5) crossed the sea; the Disciples and Jesus (6:16-21), and then the Crowds (6:22-25) crossed it back again.

But the new Discourse Moving separates Jesus from all the others, intersecting, as it were, all such horizontal movements with its own radical verticality. This Discourse Moving involves Jesus' descending from and reascending to heaven:

descending: 6:33,38,41,50,51,58 (see also 46)

reascending: 6:62.

This then becomes the primary Moving and it overshadows completely any geographical movements by Jesus or the others.

Discourse Moving among Actants

In similar fashion another and superior Moving subsumes the movements of either Crowds to Jesus or of Jesus to the Disciples. Any Moving to Jesus must be a "coming" (6:35–37,44,65) which is "given" (6:37,39) or "drawn" (6:44) or "granted" (6:65) by God. Only one who has "heard and learned from the Father comes to me" (6:45). Even more significantly, not even a choice by Jesus himself precludes this imperative: "Did I not choose you, the twelve, and one of you is a devil?" (6:70). Neither the Crowds' coming to Jesus nor Jesus' coming to the Disciples is what counts since all such Narrative Moving is controlled absolutely by a far more profound and transcendental Discourse Moving.

(b) Narrative Feeding and Discourse Feeding

The second major Narrative Action was Feeding. As one moves into Discourse one is prepared for a rather obvious parallel between feeding and teaching, between bread and revelation. This would be an obvious development of 6:1–15 (feeding, bread) and 6:16–21 (teaching, revelation). One is quite prepared for a relationship between Narrative and Discourse along the following lines. In narrative: (a) Source of Food, (b) Feeder, (c) Feeding, (d) Food, (e) Consumption of Food, (f) Consumer, (g) Bodily Life, will beget a parallelism in Discourse of: (a') Source of Revelation, (b') Revealer, (c') Revealing, (d') Revelation, (e') Belief, (f') Believer, (g') Eternal Life. But this is not at all what happens. Still, what does happen is in complete continuity with the fundamental process whereby Discourse has been steadily absorbing and consuming the Narrative and where the only Narrative element (Actants and Actions) not already thus consumed is the Narrative-Discourse Actant, the "I" of Jesus. But it would be impossible to emphasize too much the paradoxical nature of this final consumption since it is the "I" of Jesus that demands that the "I" be consumed. Thus even, or especially, here the absolute and unqualified "I AM" of 6:20 is still dominant, even over "I AM to be consumed" in 6:51–58.

The steps of the process whereby the Feeder becomes the Food are both deliberate and obvious:

The first step is 6:25–34 and the message is soothingly acceptable. God will give you the true bread from heaven which insures eternal life. What can anyone respond but: "Lord, give us this bread always" (6:34).

The second step is 6:35–48 (in a giant chiasm between 6:35a and 6:48 with the center at 6:42a) and now the Discourse turns problematic but not yet as problematic as it will be later. This bread is now identified with the "I" of Jesus. Feeder and Food are equated. The response now is murmuring and questioning (6:41–42). But the situation is not yet desperate. At this point it is still possible to hear Jesus metaphorically. If he is heavenly bread, one could see it as a metaphorical expression that he is not only Revealer (Feeder) but Revelation (Food). The call for *consumption* would still be metaphorical and would mean *acceptance* of the Revealer as the Revelation.

The third step is in 6:49–58 and it may be summarized as

6:49–50	Bread/Eat
6:51–52	I/Bread/Eat/My Flesh
6:53–56	Eat/Flesh//Drink/Blood [four times]
6:57	I/ /Eat/Me
6:58	Bread/Eat

The outer frames of 6:49–50 and 6:58 do not really go beyond the development of the second step in 6:35–48. The next inner frames of 6:51–52 and 6:57 already go beyond this by insisting outside metaphorical tolerances that the bread, which is Jesus, must be *eaten*. But it is the inner core of 6:53–56 that makes it clear that something beyond metaphor is happening. In a formulaic, hypnotic, and almost rhapsodic repetition the phrases, Eat/Flesh//Drink/Blood, move the Discourse beyond any interpretation in terms of merely *accepting* (eating) the Revealer.

I would summarize the total development so far as follows:

6:25–34	Bread
6:35–48	I/Bread
6:49–58	I/Bread/Eat Me
	Eat/My Flesh//Drink/My Blood

Two questions must now be asked. First, what is the meaning of this fourfold repetition of Eat/Flesh//Drink/Blood? Second, why is it placed precisely here in John 6?

The language of 6:49–58 is explicable only in terms of eucharistic formulae known from outside this chapter but it is even more startling than the similar formulaic repetitions in 1 Cor 11:27–29 (eat/bread//drink/cup). This furnishes four main points: it is formulaic eucharistic language; it is extremely more *realistic* than is usual elsewhere for such formulae; it is addressed to the murmuring and debating Crowds/"Jews"; it is not reacted to by them but by the Disciples among whom it causes a division (6:60–66).

It is the reaction of the Disciples that must come first in interpretation since John omits here any reaction from the Crowds/"Jews." To the murmuring Disciples Jesus says: "'Do you take offense at this? Then what if you were to see the Son of Man ascending where he was before?'" (6:61b–62). At first glance the logic of this question is not very compelling. If one presumes that *ascension* means some sort of great triumphant manifestation, then belief would be rendered easier rather than harder by witnessing it. But if ascension means crucifixion, then the logic is clarified. So also is the basic meaning of 6:51-58. Jesus is announcing there that to accept him is to accept the one who must die, who must die by the violent separation of body and blood, that is, as we shall only know later, by crucifixion. But it is also to insist that such acceptance is the only way that acceptance will ever after be possible. In other words: I am always the one to be consumed. Hence, of course, the double mention of betrayal (6:64,70-71) follows the mention of crucifixion-ascension (6:62).

Thus the primary function of the eucharistic language is to indicate a split in eucharistic understanding, that is, in the permanent acceptance of crucifixion, among the Disciples. Jesus must always be accepted as the Crucified One. What the alternative to crucifixion-eucharist might be is not indicated within this chapter (parousis-eucharist?).

But the unit in 6:51-58 is expressly addressed to the Crowds/"Jews" who do not react to it after 6:59, while the Disciples to whom it is not specifically addressed are the ones who respond to it, both negatively and positively. For John "the Jews" are those who will deny and reject the divine necessity of this crucifixional destiny and by so doing render it inevitable. *The supreme irony is that, for John, those who reject crucifixion theoretically will thereby effect it politically.* Hence, although addressed to "the Jews," their final reaction is not recorded yet. But it is reacted to immediately by some of the Disciples now because even though they will not effect the crucifixion, they will deny its permanent and enduring, that is, its eucharistic necessity.

VI. SCRIPT

This final section will, first, sum up what has happened so far, and, second, draw attention to what is the most obvious facet of the text and therefore is almost always overlooked: *it is written.*

A. TIME, SPACE, NARRATIVE, DISCOURSE

John 6 is not just composed of a simple balance of Narrative (6:1-24) whose physicality symbolizes what the succeeding Discourse (6:25-71) renders spiritual and transcendental. It is characterized by layers of text whose successive levels dominate and absorb the previous ones. In view of the text's dominant motif of eating it seems necessary to characterize this process as *consumption.*

There exists first of all the consumption of the Time, Space, Narrative, and Discourse of the Jewish Passover experience by the Time, Space, Narrative, and Discourse of a universal "Passover" phenomenon. Thus the Time of 6:4 is universalized into day-night-day and the Space sequence of crossing the sea, ascending and descending the mountain, and entering the synagogue is negated by having the sea recrossed, the mountain reascended, and the synagogue exited. The narrative of the

Feeding in 6:1–15 transcends the Exodus feeding stories as the Dialogue makes explicit in 6:31–33,49,58. And now the murmuring of the Crowds or Disciples is not about the narrative on Feeding as it was during the Exodus but about the very Discourse itself (6:41,52,60–61).

There is also, however, the consumption of the Time, Space, and Narrative of this universalized "Passover" by the Discourse which accompanies them.

Most specifically there is the consumption of the text's receiver within the collectivity of the "He Who . . ."

Finally, and most importantly, there is the consumption *by* the text's receiver (as "He Who . . .") *of* the "I" of Jesus, whose absolute "I AM" (6:20) will nevertheless transcend both "I am the bread" (6:35,48,51a) and "I am to be consumed" (6:51b–57).

B. IT IS WRITTEN

The Crowds, representing the Jewish Passover experience, and Jesus, advocating its transcendence, both invoke the biblical writings as support. In 6:31 the Crowds, talking of physical feeding, say: "*It is written*, 'He gave them bread from heaven to eat.'" And in 6:45 Jesus, speaking of spiritual feeding, says: "*It is written* in the prophets, 'And they shall all be taught by God.'" Thus the twin poles of the Discourse alike appeal to "it is written."

This central and double appeal to Scripture, and thus to *script*, force us to face what we are carefully avoiding in studying this "oral" Discourse, namely, the most obvious and therefore invisible fact about the Narrative and Discourse in John 6: *it is written*. Peter is absolutely correct in saying to Jesus: "'You have the words of eternal life'" (6:68b) but we, the readers, know them only as written, as script, and we know even Peter's oral confession only as written, as script.

At this point I am beginning to glimpse a question which renders the laborious structuralist analysis at least personally worthwhile because it has unearthed a hermeneutical issue which historical analysis did not and presumably could not uncover.

Is it of any significance that we read John 6 as *script* rather than see and hear "it" happen as event? When John 1:14 says that "the Word became flesh" and John 6:63 adds that "the flesh is of no avail," should we conclude that the Word of God became flesh and voice in order finally to become script: "the Word became script"? There, presumably, is the hermeneutical heart: is the Word of God oral or scribal or both, and, if both, are there differences and hierarchies to be maintained within that answer? Or does the Word of God have a history wherein it was originally oral and thence became scribal and what differences and hierarchies exist between such stages: oral (lost forever?), oral-scribal, and pure scribal? And is that the end of such an historical development?

At this point we can sense the questions reaching out to envelop our contemporary selves. Does it make any difference that I am asking these questions in script and your are reading them from script and how can we either ask or answer them without inevitable paradox? How could we proclaim in script the primacy of orality?

But in raising these questions I recognize that I am far from being alone. For this precise problem there is already/3/

> a community of the question, therefore, within that fragile moment when the question is not yet determined enough for the hypocrisy of an answer to have already initiated itself beneath the mask of the question, and not yet determined enough for its voice to have been already and fraudulently articulated within the very syntax of the question. A community of decision, of initiative, of absolute initiality, but also a threatened community, in which the question has not yet found the language it has decided to seek, is not yet sure of its own possibility within the community. A community of the question about the possibility of the question.

The brilliant polarities of the community of this question are represented by the writings of Walter Ong/4/ and Jacques Derrida/5/. Ong argues for the primacy of oral over scribal communication basing himself primarily on the historical primordiality of speech over script in both the species and the child. This is, however, a very dangerous argument since logically it would give an even more elevated and primordial value to the gurgle and the grunt. It is also anomalous that Ong never seems at all self-conscious in *writing* about the primacy of orality or even in citing the scripted Scriptures in support of this primordiality. Derrida, who has the advantage of a single word, *écriture*, meaning both writing and Scripture, argues for the philosophic primordiality of *écriture* since script reveals more fully, openly, and honestly the absence and deferment at the heart of the sign, of all signs of course, but which the presence of the speaker disguises in oral conversation while the absence of the writer proclaims it in scribal dialogue.

Holding, for here and now, the discussion exclusively to oral and scribal communication and bracketing the far more compelling problem of electronic communication (of Derrida one must ask: does the videotape of a dead lover reveal presence or absence, or does it, by intensifying the illusion of presence, intensify even more devastatingly the experience of absence?), I find that John 6 seems more adequately understood through Derrida than through Ong, and for two reasons.

First, if the "words" of Jesus are a mystery of spirit and life (6:63b,68), wherein what must always be consumed must always be there to be consumed anew, does this not apply more to the scribal than the oral Word of God?

Second, the Discourse in John 6 is in dialogue format and the dialogue is one of question and answer. What could be more oral than question and answer since questioner and answerer must be mutually present to one another? But these questions in John 6 seem to receive non-answers or pseudo-answers. I think this is empirically verifiable since if one lined up all the questions in one column and all their answers in another, juggled column, one could hardly line them up properly without prior knowledge of John 6. Here is the list of questions and "answers" in John 6:

Question	Answer	Non-Answer	Counter-Question
6:5		6:7	
6:9		6:10	
6:25		6:26	
6:28	6:29		
6:30 (two)		6:32–33(?)	
6:42 (two)		6:43	
6:52		6:53	
6:60			6:61–62 (two)
6:67	6:68b–69		6:68a
6:70			

There are twelve questions of which only two receive real answers; eight receive non-answers; two receive counter-questions; and one, the final word of Jesus, is a question which, in receiving no answer, terminates the Discourse. In authentic oral dialogue such "answers" would soon generate protest and demands for real answers.

Thus John 6 creates the illusion of orality and the entire Discourse proceeds through questions and pseudo-answers. The one exception is, of course, the "I AM; do not be afraid" of 6:20, but that is an exception to everything, and even that is now script and only script. Tentatively, then, John 6 moves towards this: the Word of God is script.

C. SCRIPT AND ETERNAL LIFE

Throughout 6:25-71 Jesus promises both eternal life and a raising up on the last day. "Life" is mentioned in 6:33,35,48,51,53,57,63; "eternal life" in 6:27,47,51,58,68; "raising up" in 6:39,44; and the last two terms are combined together in 6:40,54. Read together the promise is of eternal life here and now immediately as well as the promise that death will not affect the individual believer who will be raised up on the individual's last day. As used in John 6, it does not seem possible that "the last day" could refer specifically to a cosmic eschaton, else the believer would have to be "dead" for the period before its advent. But that, of course, would require further discussion in the light of the entire gospel.

But the far more important point to be noted is how the Discourse Actants are reflected in this promise. It is *never* said to anyone in John 6 by Jesus: "if *you* believe, eat, drink, etc. . . . *I* will give *you* eternal life and *I* will raise *you* up on the last day." As noted before, the Discourse "I" of Jesus subsumes all other titles and even Jesus himself, but the recipients of eternal life are not a "you" but a "he who."

And all of this endures only in script, for us here and now it endures only in script. In script, then, the Discourse "I" of Jesus remains eternally but the believer, even in script, obtains eternal life not as a personal "you" but within the community of a "he who . . ." In the words of the script, "As the living Father sent *me*, and *I* live because of the Father, so *he who* eats me will *live because of me*" (6:57).

D. GATHERING THE FRAGMENTS

I have held until last one unit of text not previously discussed but singularly striking in its emphasis. "And when they had eaten their fill, he told his disciples, 'Gather up the fragments left over, that nothing may be lost.' So they gathered them up and filled twelve baskets with fragments from the five barley loaves, left by those who had eaten" (6:12-13). It is useful at this point, as so often throughout this paper, to keep an eye on Mark, not in terms of sources but simply as a variation on the same story. Mark 6:41b-43 says: "and he divided the two fish among them all. And they all ate and were satisfied. And *they* took up twelve baskets full of broken pieces and of the fish." Note the vagueness of Mark's *they*. Thus John is very different from Mark in that he has: (1) an explicit command from Jesus to gather the fragments; (2) the command is explicitly to his disciples; (3) the reason is also given by Jesus: "that nothing may be lost"; (4) the disciples explicitly gather only the bread and not the fish. But there is something even more striking in John and that is the way these "twelve baskets" at the start of the chapter in 6:13 force a linkage with the previously unmentioned "twelve" disciples at the end of the text in 6:67-71. One therefore presumes that there is one basket for each of the twelve disciples who stay with Jesus after the others depart.

It is impossible to read the text of John, whatever about Mark, in terms of respect for either the pastoral site or the divine gift. The former would demand even greater concern for the fish fragments and the latter would demand at least equal care for both. It is only of the bread that nothing must be lost, and the bread, with the fish quietly forgotten, becomes the Discourse "I" of Jesus. It is, then, the fragments of Jesus which must be gathered so that nothing may be lost.

NOTES

/1/ Jacques Derrida, "Force et Signification," *Critique,* 193-94 (June-July 1963) was the opening essay in his *L'écriture et la différence* (Paris: Seuil, 1967), a collection of essays all, save one, published separately during 1963-1966. The collection has been translated by Alan Bass as *Writing and Difference* (Chicago: University of Chicago Press, 1978), and this opening essay, "Force and Signification" (pp. 3–30) has been reprinted in *Structuralist Review*, 1, 2 (Winter 1978), pp. 13–54. My quotation is that essay's opening sentences.

/2/   Jacques Derrida, *Writing and Difference*, p. 80.

/3/   I am aware that the terms Narrative (deeds) and Discourse (words) are not entirely satisfactory. They may cause confusion with the much more technical distinctions between Story (the content, the what) and Discourse (the expression, the how) suggested by Seymour Chatman, *Story and Discourse: Narrative Structure in Fiction and Film* (Ithaca, NY: Cornell University Press, 1978). I have not been able to adapt Chatman's excellent categories to John 6 (although it may well be possible to do so with future study) primarily because of the very special relationship between what Jesus does (my Narrative) and what Jesus says (my Discourse) in John 6. But, for future reference, see Chatman's section on (his term) "Discourse" (pp. 146–262) and especially his comment that, "When we know more about textual and semantic analysis, it may be possible to develop viable taxonomies of dialogue types" (p. 177). He cites Maurice Blanchot's three-way distinction of dialogue, exemplified from Malraux, James and Kafka, and notes that, "Kafka's characters, for their part, are doomed forever to talk at cross-purposes, past each other" (p. 178). The application of that concept to the "non"-dialogue in John 6 is quite obvious.

/4/   Walter J. Ong, *The Presence of the Word* (New Haven, CT: Yale University Press, 1967); *Rhetoric, Romance and Technology* (Ithaca, NY: Cornell University Press, 1971); *Interfaces of the Word* (Ithaca, NY: Cornell University Press, 1977). A magnificent section of that last book, pp. 230–71, has been reprinted as "Maranatha: Death and Life in the Text of the Book," *JAAR*, 45 (December 1977), pp. 419–49.

/5/   Besides the collection noted in the first footnote above, see also, "White Mythology: Metaphor in the Text of Philosophy," *New Literary History*, 6 (1974), pp. 5–74; and *Of Grammatology*, trans. by Gayatri Chakravorty Spivak (Baltimore, MD: The Johns Hopkins University Press, 1976).

"THIS IS A HARD SAYING. WHO CAN BE LISTENER TO IT?": CREATING A READER IN JOHN 6

Gary A. Phillips
Holy Cross College

Precis

The purpose of this essay is to offer a reading of John 6 in terms of its nature and function as discourse and its capacity to create a reader. In particular, our effort will be to describe the text of John 6 as an instance of enunciation (*énonciation*)/1/, of speaking, whose signifying effect is one of fashioning its reader through the interplay of different levels and types of speaking that take place within the text. This constructive effect is the result of the interaction of text with reader, who, though in one sense presupposed by the very fact of communication, assumes a specific kind of reading role structured by the interplay of different enunciative relationships (at the level of the text as a whole, the narrator and the narrative characters) unfolding within the text. In the case of John 6 the reading role emerges from an iconic patterning between the type of speaking/hearing that occurs within the text (among the narrative characters and narrator) and the speaking/reading of the Evangelist's discourse as a whole.

I. THE THEORETICAL AND METHODOLOGICAL FRAMEWORK OF OUR READING: DISCOURSIVIZATION

Our framework for reading John 6 is one that is concerned with the dimension of signification which Charles Morris identified as *pragmatics*/2/. A notion which traces its way back to the American philosopher-semiotician Charles Sanders Peirce, pragmatics has been associated traditionally with the study of (1) the relationship between the sign or signifier of meaning and its world of reference, and (2) more particularly the process of semeiosis by which the sign relates to its recipient, in the case of John 6 the flesh and blood reader/hearer of the text. An interest in the pragmatics of John 6 as text, however, does not diminish the importance of syntactic and semantic investigations of the text (two correlates which along with pragmatics constitute the sign's triadic structure). Morris makes it clear, as does Peirce before him, that a comprehensive reflection upon the sign demands a consideration of all three dimensions—syntactics, semantics and pragmatics. In our case, concern for the pragmatics of the text reflects a methodological choice to bring into view an oft-neglected but crucial dimension of the text that helps to explain the creative relationship of the text as a sign to its reader.

The choice of a pragmatic approach, however, becomes polemical for certain structuralist and semiotic exegetes who for epistemological reasons privilege syntactic and semantic models and methods to the exclusion of pragmatic methods and models/3/. So long as the preference for the syntactics and semantics of the text reflects a strategy for reading and is thus a methodological choice (the result, perhaps, of more fully developed syntactic and, to a lesser extent, semantic models in linguistics and communication theory), the issue is essentially one of approach. However, when syntactic and semantic preference is asserted in a fundamental way, epistemological differences in the understanding of sign, semeiosis and text are at issue. For instance, the sign is viewed *statically* as opposed to being viewed *dynamically*; semeiosis is a discontinuous and encapsulated process as opposed to an on-going and open-ended process; text is an object of reader appropriation rather than an event of involvement in which the reader comes into being/4/.

Our approach presupposes a dynamic view of the nature and function of sign and of the text as an instance of sign. From the semiotic perspective of Peirce, the sign and signification process may be viewed in triadic terms: each and every sign is made up of signifier/representamen, object and interpretant. And since each aspect of the sign is defined in terms of its structural relationships, a sign belongs to an on-going semiotic process by which it can become an interpretant or object or signifier for some other sign in some other signifying relationship/5/. Consequently, with Peirce we can say that

> a sign, or representamen, is something which stands to somebody for something in some respect or capacity. It addresses somebody, that is creates in the mind of that person a more developed sign. That sign which it creates I call the *interpretant* of the first sign. The sign stands for something, its *object*. It stands for that object, not in all respects but in reference to a sort of idea, which I have sometimes called the *ground* of the representamen/6/.

Applying Peirce's notion of sign to the text of John 6, we can say that it is a sign for somebody in some respect or capacity, addressing somebody and creating in the mind of that person a more developed sign, or interpretant, of the text. This is a *process* of sign production which, we must not forget, is itself situated within a matrix of signifying relationships that is in flux, perpetually forming and provoking different signs and different interpretants for ever new hearers or readers. As a result of the dynamic nature of the signifying process we are justified in speaking of the text as engaged in a *creative process* in relation to its reader through the particular semiotic role or capacity it offers the readers as sign recipient to be engaged in the creation of the text as a *meaningful-sign-for-the-reader*. The reader in this way becomes in some sense both benefactor and product of the sign, both the creator of the text and at the same time created by the text. It is the hearer/reader's intimate involvement in the process of the text's coming-to-meaning that makes Peirce's sign theory suggestive for understanding the interpretative process.

From a less semiotic and more traditional hermeneutic perspective, P. Ricoeur has argued for a similar understanding of text as process. For him the text's goal is to construct a discourse and for this purpose it presupposes a speaker, a world and a vis-a-vis. The text is a discursive *work*, a linguistic productivity in which there is a reference backward to a speaker and a communicative relationship with some listener/reader. In short, in order for the text (as discourse) to be text it must be rooted in a dynamic communicative process and relationship in which text and reader are brought together, an effect is produced and a textual world (an interpretant) is created in contradistinction to the "real" world (in fact, itself an interpretant) which exists prior to the engagement of reader and text. We will have more to say about the two worlds and their relationship to one another below.

John 6 offers an excellent text for the study of enunciative structure for reasons that are important to both traditional (historical) and nontraditional (i.e., structural and semiotic) criticism. Traditionally identified as the Evangelist's "Bread of Life Discourse," this chapter has lent itself to a division into discursive and narrative parts. Reflecting the influence of a source critical orientation, this segmentation of the chapter focuses upon textual units defined primarily in terms of textual form and function. The end result is often a gross separation of vv 1-26 (Feeding of the Multitude; the Journey to the Lake) from vv 27-59 (the Bread of Life Discourse proper)/7/. Even from a redaction critical perspective, narrative and discursive parts are separated in spite of the attempt to discover an overall narrative coherence and purpose in the chapter. Either the narrative pericopes (the Multiplication of Bread, Walk upon Water) are taken to be illustrative of the meaning of the discourse on bread, or conversely the discourse is seen to expand and interpret the narrative segments in discursive form.

A reading that forces a distinction between narrated events and discourse maintains the structure of individual pericopes at the expense of the larger textual units and structures (minimally the chapter as a whole).

Curiously, the distinction which is so important at the level of the chapter as a whole is blurred within the supposedly narrative segments themselves where narrative figures engage in speaking behavior (e.g., 6:5–12). By contrast, the segmentation and enunciative reading that we propose divides the text in a different way and proposes an overall structure that redefines the relationship of narrative verse with discoursive verse in view of explaining the relationship between text and reader.

A certain type of structural exegesis is subject to the same criticism though it operates its segmentation from an altogether different methodological starting point. Structural exegesis' tendency to work with short, mostly narrative, textual units betrays its interest in syntactic as opposed to pragmatic structures. There is, however, a growing concern among certain structuralist critics to treat larger units of text and to consider semantic and pragmatic dimensions of the text/8/. In this sense, a reading attuned to enunciative structure responds to weaknesses associated with historico-critical and structuralist approaches.

Finally, with a description of the enunciative character of John 6 we can begin to provide an explanation of the *event quality* of John 6 as text. If, as Speech Act theorists maintain, language does more than merely state what is the case in the world (its referential or constative function)—i.e., it transforms, enacts, performs (its performative function) or creates a *world*—then attention must be paid to developing systematic ways of speaking about the performative nature of the text as language. Presuming that the language of John 6 in its textual form qualifies as a special instance of language working or enacting, attention to the character of the enunciation that is narrated *within* the chapter may be instrumental in understanding how the enunciation *of* the text as a whole is to be explained. For this reason our reading strategy is to search out the different levels of enunciation as they are presented in or presupposed by the text. If as linguists, communication theorists and semioticians tell us the phenomenon of linguistic enunciation can be described in terms of the categories related to the speaking subject and recipient (enunciator and enunciatee, respectively), the temporal and spatial character of the speaking and the particular mode of relationship between the speaking (modus) and that which is spoken (dictum or utterance), then attending to the conditions of enunciation as they are manifested within John 6 will lead us in the direction of a pragmatic description of John's text.

In this way we can see how the text works to create a textual world and the specific speaking/hearing roles that populate that space. It is the interpenetration (*imbrication*) of these enunciative structures, specifically of the narrative characters, the recipient of the narrator's speaking and the recipient of the textual speaking (implied reader)/9/ which contributes to John 6's distinctive meaning effect and its power to engage and create new readers. This enunciative interpenetration is key to the text's performative power in establishing an "implied reader" who enters into the narrative world of John's narrative text as one of Jesus' discoursive partners, a "you" who dialogues with Jesus the actor, with John the narrator and with the text itself. In this way, the text as sign is responsible for fashioning its readership through the narrativizing of the text's implied reader enunciation *as an icon of the narrative of Jesus* engaged in different manners of speaking.

A. ENUNCIATION, UTTERANCE AND ENUNCIATIVE MARKERS

In order to situate our understanding of the process of enunciation in John 6 and to describe the different conditions of enunication let us return to Greimas's definition as proposed in his *Dictionary*. Enunciation is the general act of producing discourse. This discoursive act may be described in either of two ways: from the point of view of the *process* or means of production of discourse; or from the point of view of these utterances as the discoursive *product* of that act (the text produced)/10/. In the former instance we focus upon the conditions which presuppose and lead to the production of the text; in the latter, upon the message which is produced. This distinction between process and product is, however, ultimately artificial and is intended to serve a propadeutic function in enabling the critic to focus upon different dimensions of the complex phenomenon of sign production and meaning.

By focusing upon the conditions of enunciation, in particular the categories of enunciator (the subject "I" who produces the utterance) and enunciatee (the "you" or recipient of the utterance), we can provide a framework for segmenting the text and for structuring the various types and levels of discoursive roles and interrelationships found within the text. In John 6 this leads us to identify three different enunciative relationships or levels:

(1) *The level of textual enunciation.* Comparable to Chatmann's level of "implied sender" and "implied reader," the textual enunciation is presupposed by John 6 and the entire Gospel. The textual enunciation is to be distinguished from the *scriptive* enunciation (the physical production/reception of the text) in that the former is a role presupposed explicitly for John 6 as text and constitutes the unifying force and organizing point of view behind the text.

(2) *The level of narrational enunciation.* The narration is that necessary enunciation which functions as the textual speaking and perspective through which the narrative events unfold. Both narrator and narratee (the narrational "I" and "you" of the narrated events discourse, respectively) may assume different modes of presence or absence (e.g., covert or overt, proximate or distant) with respect to the textual

enunciation and narrative enunciation within the text. For example, the narrational enunciation may be dissimulated within the text in the speaking of the characters located within the narrative events themselves. Regardless, however, of the mode of manifestation, narrational enunciation is necessarily presupposed by the narrative events.

(3) *The level of actorial enunciation.* Here we locate specific discourse on the part of characters who engage in speaking behavior within the narrated events themselves. Just as the narrator/narratee and textual enunciator/textual enunciatee engage in discoursive acts, so too the actors who populate the narrative world of the text (e.g., Jesus and the disciples at different moments assume the enunciative roles of "I" and "you") may speak in a multitude of different ways.

An identification of the various levels of enunciation and their relationship to one another provides us with an important means for describing the unifying force of John 6 and the effect achieved by the text of John as a process of textual production. An enunciation at one level of the text may be superimposed upon an enunciative relationship at another level (e.g., Jesus' speaking is taken over as the narrator's speaking). This enunciative overlapping is made possible by the empty or open-ended character of the enunciative markers (indicators of enunciative subjectivity, temporality, spatiality and modality) present in the utterance as sedimentations of the enunciative process which has yielded the utterance as a discourse. As we will see, the nature of the narrational and actorial enunciative relationship is a crucial factor in determining the overall effect achieved by the text. In the case of John 6 narrational and actorial enunciation are related *iconically*: the speaking/hearing at the actorial level is reflected and refracted in the speaking/hearing at the narrational level; furthermore, the narrational level is reflected at the level of the textual enunciation. This capacity of the text owes in part to the perpetual openness of the enunciative markers as signs which project ever different interpretants or meanings. It is the openendedness of these enunciative markers and their capacity to signify in an ambiguous way *different* enunciative relationships that makes it possible for a reader to "enter" into a text as a discoursive partner of Jesus, to become a participant in the narrational enunciation or to become the implied receiver of the text which the textual enunciative strategy is aimed at producing. Enunciative ambiguity and superposition prove to be fundamental features of this text's semiotic potential/11/.

To summarize by way of illustration we may represent the various enunciative relationships as follows:

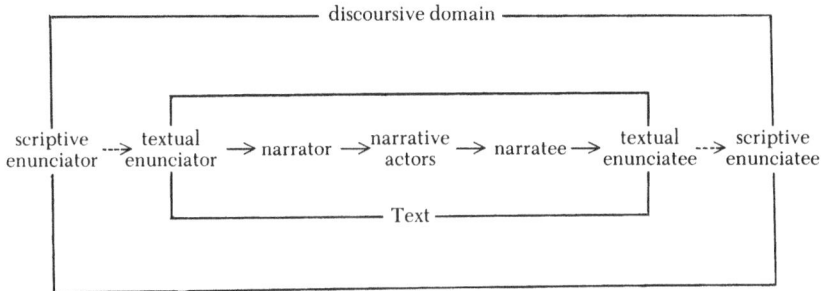

Textual Enunciative Roles

Applying the model to John 6 we produce the following model of enunciative relationships:

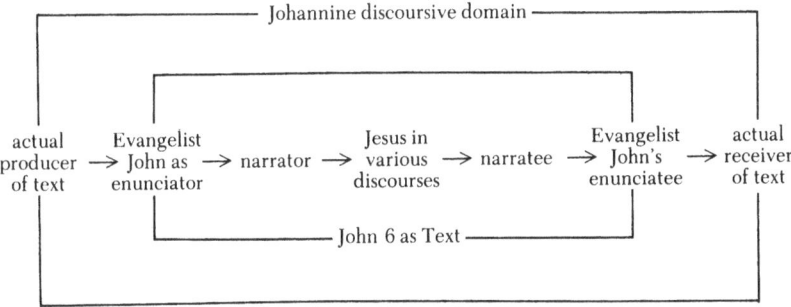

Textual Enunciative Roles in John 6

In this model of John 6 we can see how easy it is to confuse the scriptive enunciator with the textual enunciator or the narrating voice within the text. While an overlapping of enunciative positions may occur it need not necessarily take place. Indeed, failure to perceive this distinction has led redaction critics, for example, to identify scriptive speaking with narrational speaking and has produced an unwarranted confidence that the historical reconstruction of the former is possible through the literary consideration of the latter. While a certain degree of reconstruction is indeed possible, the text critic must first recognize the world of the text (the reality as interpretant of the textual enunciation) and the variety of relationships and strategies that exist between textual, narrational and actorial enunciation. At the very least semiotic and structuralist criticism shows that the world of the text is not to be identified without remainder with the world presupposed *by* the text and lying in some sense outside of it. Given John's text as our starting point we need first to reconstruct the world and values articulated *within* the text before we can speak of the world that gave rise to such a text, to such a possibility of speaking, in the first place.

While we have to distinguish between the world of the text and the world lying before the text, at the same time we have to acknowledge, following Peirce, their common semiotic nature. The character of both *textual* and *extratextual* worlds as interpretants or signs points to the perfusive nature of signs—all things are signs—and all signs are part of an ongoing sign sending, sign producing, sign receiving process. The perfusion of signs forces us to recognize that the world of John's text and the world which the historical critic seeks to reconstruct from John's text are equally the production of semeiosis. The former in that sense is no less real than the latter. Consequently, the traditional distinction between textual and extra-textual, fictional and real, is subject to revision in semiotic terms. If semiotic criticism leads to a reassessment of the fundamental literary categories employed by the biblical critic, then the objection raised by many historico-critical scholars that structural/semiotic criticism has nothing to contribute to the historico-critical understanding of the text is overstated.

B. DISCOURSE AND ENUNCIATIVE MARKERS

The act of enunciation is responsible for the creation of a certain class of signs whose very existence and significance is dependent upon the act of speaking, or in the case of John 6, of textual production/12/. Among those signs are included indicators of subjectivity (e.g., personal and possessive pronouns), temporality (e.g., temporal adverbs, verbal tense markers), spatiality (e.g., demonstrative pronouns) and modality (qualifiers like "perhaps," "no doubt," etc.). In addition to particular lexical signs the enunciation leaves its mark at the level of the sentence and beyond the sentence in a variety of syntactical features, notably interrogatory and imperatival formations and supra-sentential modalizations expressive of the *modus* of the enunciator's relationship to the enunciatee through the utterance formation and function.

According to the linguist-communication theorist Eugene Nida, all discourse displays a number of universal characteristics: two of these characteristics relate to the discourse as a whole (markers of beginning and end; transitional markers of internal division of the entire discourse); three relate to the events contained within the discourse proper (markers of temporal relation, spatial relation and logical relation); two relate to objects within the discourse (identification of discoursive participation); and one relates to the author (markers of attitude or point of view).

Nida's eight universal categories may be reduced to the four deictic categories of subjectivity, temporality, spatiality, and modality elaborated by Jakobson, Benveniste and others/13/. In the broadest sense, deictics (from *deichnymi*, meaning "to point," "to indicate") is an umbrella term for those formal properties (*formalen Eigenschaften von Ausserungen*) of the enunciative act. Since deictics are signifiers of the particular discoursive circumstances or conditions which make an utterance possible, deictics prove to be an important clue to an understanding of the enunciation and of the pragmatic effect of John's text.

Those formal properties which condition the possibility of a text are coded directly into language: subject deixis (*Personaldeixis*) signals the status, function and value of the subjects (both sender and receiver) in discourse; temporal deixis (*Zeitdeixis*), the time in which the enunciation unfolds; spatial deixis (*Ortdeixis*), the spatial relationship of the subjects of the discourse engaged in the process of communication; and modal deixis (*Rededeixis*), the attitude of the discursive subjects in relation to one another vis-a-vis the utterance/14/.

(1) *Subjectivity*

Subject deixis is manifested in discourse primarily through pronoun structure and verbal inflection, though Benveniste has shown that the same function can be met kenetically through body positioning and movement. According to Benveniste, markers of subjectivity not only indicate the presupposed enunciative partners to the discourse (Peirce's "somebody" for whom something can be a sign) but most importantly make it possible even to speak of person or subject at all. For "it is in and by language that man is constituted as subject. . . . Subjectivity is the capacity for the speaker to situate himself as subject"/15/. Moreover, the intersubjective character of discourse is to be explained in the functional and reversible nature of the enunciative roles: speaker (enunciator) can become hearer (enunciatee) and vice-versa. The two roles, however, are not identical; they are hierarchically related in that the "I" stands in an oriented relationship vis-a-vis the "you" and controls the flow of the discourse/16/: the "I" affects the "you" in and through the speaking. This vis-a-vis of speaker and hearer signals the manipulative and performative power of discourse.

In addition to the vis-a-vis of enunciator and enunciatee we can also speak of the vis-a-vis of subject and world (or non-subject) as reflected grammatically in the contrast between first and second person pronouns and third person pronouns. Whereas first and second person pronouns signify an intersubjective relationship, the third person pronoun signifies the non-subject, that which is other. Thus the pronominal structure of language indicates the very subjective conditions of discourse in which subject and world come to be and to be related in language.

The relationship of subject to subject and subject to world is made clear in another way when we attempt to delineate the respective objects or referents of these "discursive" and "non-discursive" pronouns/17/. The ultimate object of the discursive pronouns is the very act of enunciation itself in which the subject comes to be in and through the discourse; they refer neither to concepts nor to individuals but to discursive roles, to enunciative *roles*. Unlike the third person pronoun which signifies a reality projected outside of the discursive relationship as a result of the enunciation/18/ (note, however, that the "non-discoursive reality" is nonetheless an interpretant), discoursive pronouns indicate enunciative roles. They are, as Morris says, *pragmatic* signs for which no single class of referents exists. Indeed it would not be inappropriate to say that there is no independent reality which stands outside of the moment of discourse in which they are used in the same way that there is no object which stands outside of a semiotic relationship from which it derives its status as a sign.

We can now see why the pronominal system serves as a primary locus for identifying the enunciation within text and for speaking of subjectivity in language. Establishing the subject and the intersubjective relationship provides a framework for speaking of both the discoursive relationship between speaker and hearer and also of the non-discoursive relationship between speaker/hearer and world. Applied to a reading of John 6 the identification of subject deixis helps us to locate the different enunciators and enunciatees and the different levels of enunciation as well as the powerful ambiguity of these signs in signifying one or more discoursive relationships at a given time. Attention to subject deixis allows us to focus upon the speaking subjects in the text and leads us to ask, Who speaks in the unfolding of the narrrative events? Who enunciates these events? Who is the hearer/reader of these words? How do the various kinds of speaking affect the "you" who is recipient of John 6?

(2) *Temporality*

Like subjectivity, temporality forms an innate cadre of language and of text/19/. Not only does enunciation generate and indicate the subject within language, enunciation is also responsible for establishing the temporal character (present, past or future) of that discoursive presence. Enunciation is responsible then for what we as readers experience as "time" within a text. Attention to markers of speaking/hearing time and the relation of enunciating time to the time projected out of it (the time of the narrative events or utterance time) will help us to orient the enunciative relationships within the text and to explain the way in which the reader is "caught up within the story."

In grammatical terms "tense" (the *time* of the verb) proves to be the primary linguistic mode by which the temporal character of enunciation is manifested in discourse. The time of the verb designates not only temporality but also communicates a particular mode of relationship between the one who speaks and that which is said (between the enunciation proper and the utterance produced). Benveniste and others have recognized that tense is the *means* by which the enunciating "I" and "you" come into being in discourse in a discoursive "now" while at the same time projecting a non-discoursive presence outside of the speaking ("he," "she," "they") in a time other than now ("then")/20/.

The recognition that the enunciative moment generates the "present" of the language as well as the "non-present" associated with the utterance has led to an attempt to develop a typology of text types on the basis of whether the text manifests explicit references to the time of the enunciation or to the time of the narrative events themselves (cf. Todorov's classic distinction between the *"temps du discours"* versus the *"temps de l'histoire"*). On the basis of the distinction between enunciating time and narrative time Benveniste concluded that those texts which employ a certain group of tenses have the enunciator and enunciatee present while other texts featuring the alternative tense system lacked any enunciative subject. Unfortunately, Benveniste's attempt to correlate tense system with text type failed to recognize that *every* text or utterance, regardless of its mode of expression, by definition presupposes an enunciative subject insofar as the text is a speaking. Thus it is not a question of lack of enunciative subjects but of the text's mode of manifestation of the enunciator/enunciatee. Non-manifestation of the *markers* of enunciative subject ought not to be taken then as a sign of the lack of enunciation but as a deliberate choice of the mode of expression. Consequently, Benveniste's attempt to construct a typology of text types on the basis of tense system and correlation with enunciative presence or absence fails. Rather, tense system is part of a deliberate selection (as a result of generic and other socio-semiotic constraints) of communicative form, strategy of production and meaning effect. The suppression of markers of enunciative presence either in the form of subject or of temporal deictics contributes to the effect of bringing the non-subject and the time-other-than-now to the forefront. Expressed in terms of the text of John 6, the narrative events become the focus of attention and the reader's gaze is shunted away from the textual enunciative subject and time which presupposes the production of the narrative events.

The relationship of the time of enunciation (the discoursive "now") to the time of the utterance (the "time-other-than-now" projected in the text) functions in a complex and semiotically rich way within a narrative which portrays an enunciating or speaking and a textual time projected further within the narrative folds of the text/21/. Just as a text may have an englobing subjective presence (a narrating "I" who speaks as a narrative figure who is an "I" within the text behind which stands the "I" of the textual enunciator), so a text can also present an englobing of different enunciative "nows" and "thens." It is the deictic character of language that makes it possible to present the process of enunciation at multiple levels and allows it to become a textual device (as for example in the story of *A Thousand and One Nights* and *The Canterbury Tales*) in which the present time and speaking of the narrating subject and the time and speaking of the narrative actors are superimposed: the now of the narrating and the then—which becomes a now of the actors—overlap and interpenetrate.

Of the various temporal expressions of enunciation, the present tense stands out as that special form of time indicator in which the enunciation is most easily recognized and the process of "entering" the time of the speaking most readily apparent/22/. The function of the present in narrative text is often contrastive, a way to distinguish between the time and non-presence projected as a correlate in the utterance. While the effort to identify a so-called "narrative" tense (see the discussion regarding the epic preterite)/23/, like Benveniste's effort, mistakenly attempted to correlate tense form with literary genre rather than with enunciative level, function, and effect. The recognition of the close connection between speaking and the present tense calls for closer description.

In the case of the preterite tense in narrative literature, the function is not to assign a time sphere to a given type of literature but to "fictionalize" events, to present them as forming a narrative world, in other words to *create* a narrative time, subject and place. The preterite points, then, in an oblique way to the "*Aussagesubjekt*": "it enables us to differentiate between the words and thoughts of the implied author (or textual enunciator) on the one hand and of a fictional or projected character on the other." Tense form is another expression of the relationship between the subject and her communication which becomes at certain moments in history singled out as a special literary code.

Within this framework it is now possible to explain the function of the so-called historical present. Like the deictics of subject which function simultaneously at different speaking levels, the present tense can indicate a multitude of different speaking times (1) because it reaffirms the indexical character of the present tense as sign and (2) underscores the interpretative nature of the different enunciative levels. The historical present contributes in no small way to the interpenetration of discoursive relationship.

The historical present, or unhistorical present as labeled ironically by Jespersen/24/, enables the speaker to project self outside of the enunciating context and into the narrative. To use the metaphor of levels, the narrator speaks in the present tense in order to move from the narrating time and space into the narrated time and space of the text. This presencing effect (*vergegenwärtigende Wirkung*)/25/ has long been noted by grammarians as a way of including the reader within the set of narrative events. Along with the aorist, the historical present is used in "vivid narratives at the events which the narrator imagines himself to be present"/26/. This ambiguous referential function (both inside and outside of the narrative) enables the reader to take his stand with the textual enunciator, narrator and actor in the midst of the moving panorama of the narrative. Because of the semiotic openendedness of temporal deictics, the use of the present tense gives us another way to account for the "realism of the narrative" and the textual effect of "entrapping the reader within the story."

(3) *Spatiality*

Like temporality and subjectivity, spatiality is a necessary product of enunciation. Speaking generates spatializaion and with it the sense of a world of reference both with respect to the world "inside" language (or text) and the world which precedes or stands outside the text/27/. From a grammatical point of view the language of a text works at locating speaking/hearing through the use of prepositions, demonstrative pronouns and adverbs of place, proper nouns and place names and other indicators of *Ortdeixis*, in order both to establish a relationship between speaking subjects and a world of reference and to create the sense of a world outside of the text. It is this referential functioning of language which arises in the enunciation process of engaging and disengaging the speaking/hearing subjects within discourse.

Reference to world (spatialization), then, is basic to the functioning of language: it is language's capacity to function in a supremely indexical fashion by designating what is other. Such an understanding of the creative power of speaking to create a world through reference means that "world" or "reality" does not designate some univocal, objective world lying outside and before all discourse and signification. Rather, reality or world whether inside or outside of the text is an *effect* of language, a function of sign used deictically or indexically/28/. Text is that special literary sign whose function it is to draw literary attention to a world and the world-creating capacity of linguistic signs.

The capacity of language to refer (what Peirce calls the Secondness of the sign) is an essential aspect of the sign and its structure. Traditionally associated with the issue of the pragmatics of language, linguists have bracketed both the matter of reference and the larger question of pragmatics for methodological and epistemological reasons. The argument is that (1) language is essentially symbolic in nature and (2) a description of language in pragmatic terms is an impossible task given the complex forces and constraints that lead to language production. Yet, Peirce's triadic sign theory removes this objection (1) by showing that the symbolic (the Thirdness of the sign) is but one of three different, mutually implicatory categories of sign functions and (2) by underscoring the perfusive nature of signs, namely that the relationship of language to world is *fundamentally* semiotic and definable, at least from Peirce's point of view, in terms of sign, sign relation and sign structure. Thus, to describe the situation of discourse which gives rise to language (the world to which language refers) is in effect to identify the *conditions* and *character* of the world as sign.

Turning to John 6 as text, spatialization is an enunciative effect conditioned by the production of the text as sign. The world to which John 6 refers is a meaning effect constituted by its speaking/hearing (both in and of the text); its reality (the narrative actors, their actions and words, the narrative's believability as a time and place, a "world") is a result of the sign within and of the text as a whole to function indexically and to situate a speaking/hearing subject vis-a-vis that world through the use of those signs. By attending to the nature and distribution of spatial deictics in John 6 not only can we describe the narrative world of reference within which Jesus acts and speaks, we can speak of the world presupposed by this narrative world and its relationship to the enunciator who as narrator utters it and who stands in a certain relationship to that world from the point of view of another temporal and spatial locus. The nature of this relationship as narrated through the markers of the narrator's absence/presence in spatial, temporal and subjective terms within the world of the narrative events contributes to the overall effect of the text and the kind of world lying outside of and before the text.

(4) *Modalization*

Modality is a fourth enunciative condition. A logico-linguistic concept, modality in language signals "that qualification of logical presuppositions according to which they are distinguished as asserting or denying the possibility, impossibility, contingency or necessity of their content"/29/. Underlying this notion is the distinction proposed by logicians between the representative content of an utterance (dictum) and the attitude (modus) of the speaking subject with regard to its content. Already implying the presence and relationship of utterance to subject of enunciation, modality has to do with the interpretative shape given to the utterance and the character of the speaking subject's presence in relation to the utterance. As a creative effect achieved by the enunciation/30/, modalization situates the intentionality or purpose of the speaking subject in relation to what is said within the text.

Modal indices may be manifested in a variety of forms including adverbs of opinion ("perhaps," "apparently"), temporal adverbs, syntactic formulations (e.g., use of emphatic and passive constructions, reported versus reporting speech patterns, so-called "presentatifs" ("here," "now"), rhetorical patterning, chiastic constructions, illocutionary and perlocutionary forces, etc./31/. The identification of modal indices is an important element in describing the pragmatic effect of language. An indicator of the subjective interrelationship and subject-world relationship, attention to modal features can provide important clues to the speaking strategy and the effect intended by a certain speaking both at the level of the narrative and textual enunciation.

In the case of John 6, the identification of modal signs helps us to explain the nature of the different discursive relationships that exist in the text between Jesus and the other actors, between the narrator and Jesus. For instance, the exchange between Jesus and the people (6:10) is interpreted by the narrator as "testing." The narrator's intention is to interpret the meaning of the disciples' speaking with an indicator of the disciples' intention with respect to their speaking. In this way the narrator's intention vis-a-vis his/her presupposed reader/hearer is communicated: namely, to reveal a degree of comprehension of and distance from the narrative events on the narrator's part that leaves the narratee in the position of knowing what is "true" or "false," "secret" or "misleading" about the events at the narrative level.

In John 6 the interaction of modal, subjective, temporal and spatial deictics constitutes the pragmatic effect of establishing a reliable and knowledgeable narratee. The distance of the narrator to the narrative events is communicated by way of an absence/presence of narrational enunciation. The proximity of the narrator to the narrative events situates the narratee within the flow of the narrative events—and, in the case of John 6, of the narrative's various discourses; the absence of the narrational deictics separates narratee from the narrative events.

In turning to a description of enunciation in John 6 we want to show the way in which the text constitutes a strategy for understanding the discourse of Jesus by providing a program by which the text equips its reader to understand what "discourse with Jesus" means and also pragmatically to create a competence on the part of the reader in discoursing with Jesus. In other words, by attending to the enunciative relationships we can describe John 6 as proclamatory and parenetic in two respects: through John 6 the narrator says what Jesus is (bread = word) and how Jesus is (miracle working and miracle speaking) and also what the disciple is (an adequate discourse partner) and how he/she can be that way (as modeled after Simon Peter's speaking). The text's work is to proclaim and to produce.

II. READING THE TEXT

A. SEGMENTATION OF THE TEXT

The text suggests a criterion for its segmentation in the manner in which it presents different narrative figures engaged in discourse with Jesus. The intentional selection of discourse structure as a key to division and subsequent reading of the text contrasts with other types of segmentation (either narrative verse/discursive verse or simple verse by verse segmentation). Our approach, like traditional modes of segmenting the text, organizes the text in accordance with a particular set of presuppositions. Our discursive segmentation simply makes overt the process that is covert and presupposed by traditional exegetes in their reading of the text.

Our procedure will be to examine the text discursively at three different levels: that of the narrative events level (actorial enunciation), the narrational level (narrational enunciation) and textual level (textual enunciation)/32/. The focus of our attention will be primarily on the first two levels and the interplay of the narrator's speaking strategy and presentation of the narrative events with the narrative events themselves. An adequate description of the textual enunciation requires a more complete consideration of the values presupposed not only in John 6 but in the rest of the Gospel than can be provided in this essay.

B. NARRATIVE EVENTS LEVEL

At this level we seek to organize the text in terms of the various discoursive exchanges and relationships between Jesus and other actors in the chapter. In the text Jesus is presented in discourse with the following figures:

DISCOURSE #	VERSES	PERSONAGE(S)
1	6:1–13	Philip, Andrew, disciples
2	6:14–15	crowd
3	6:16–21	his disciples
4	6:22–40	crowd
5	6:41–58	Jews
6	6:59–65	many disciples
7	6:66–71	Simon Peter, Twelve

An examination of Jesus' discursive behavior reveals that he addresses two kinds of enunciatees: (1) a distinct group with specified spokespersons (e.g., Philip, Andrew and disciples; Simon Peter and Twelve); and (2) an ill-defined group with unspecified speakers (crowd; Jews; many disciples). As we will see when describing the narrational discursive level, the order and nature of these different enunciative partners suggests a strategy in the effect created both with respect to the narratee (and ultimately with the implied reader of the text). The chiastic movement of distinct to ill-defined/ill-defined to distinct speaking partners functions as a discursive device in the narrator's manipulation of the narratee through the course of the narrative events.

The proposed segmentation in terms of enunciative relationships reveals the *inclusio* character of vv 1–13 (DIS 1) and 66–71 (DIS 7). Bracketing is accomplished with the reference to Simon Peter, the disciples, the Twelve (disciples and baskets) and the parallel insertion of the narrator's voice with the interpretative comments ("This he said to test him; Jesus knew what he meant to do"; and "He meant Judas son of Simon Iscariot. He it was who would betray him, and he was one of the Twelve"). In both instances the presence of the narrating subject's voice within the narrative events is important in the manipulation of events on the narrator's part.

In the first discourse (DIS 1) Jesus' enunciative position is marked spatially by reference to his being "on the further side of the Sea of Galilee," specifically on a "hill-side"; and temporally it is "near the time of the Passover." The discoursive partners are Jesus (included in the first person "we") and Philip, Andrew and the disciples (the "you" implied by Jesus' "we"). The modality of intention communicated in Jesus' speaking to the disciples is to "test" which is communicated to the reader by way of the narrator's description-interpretation ("This he said to test him"). In this narrative exchange Jesus unmistakably directs the flow of the discoursive events with a question that entraps the disciples by involving them in the role of "we"—"Where are *we* to buy bread and to feed these people?" Jesus fails to respond either to Philip's response or to Andrew's question and instead underscores his own control of the discoursive exchange with double imperative ("Make them sit down"; "Collect the pieces left over"). Not only is the disciples' ability to engage in discourse with Jesus defined on Jesus' terms, there is also no identification by way of response to Philip or to Andrew's words regarding the location or source of the bread.

In DIS 2 the enunciative context changes. Now the people attempt to come and to speak with Jesus. But discourse with Jesus does not take place on the people's terms (just as it did not take place on Philip's and Andrew's terms in DIS 1) as indicated in the following ways: (1) The people are cast as the enunciator "I" while Jesus occupies a non-discoursive or third person role; (2) the people are described as speaking to others as opposed to speaking with Jesus; and (3) Jesus communicates his refusal to speak by going away. Jesus is still manipulating the discoursive possibilities. The crowd acclaims Jesus as "the prophet that was to come into the world" in response to what has immediately transpired in the feeding narrative. But Jesus' refusal to speak is tantamount to his refusal of this identification at this time not for the reason, as the narrator will make clear, that the people are wrong in their identification; on the contrary, the people are right but for the wrong reasons. Only after Jesus interprets the Scriptures and teaches (discourse on the Scriptures, DIS 7) is his identity fully unmasked (6:51). Jesus is thus prophet not just in deed but in *WORD* as well. Expressed in terms of the modality of their speaking, the intention on the part of the crowd is to "proclaim him King," to speak *to* him, to take charge by way of language and not to come and listen and thus become hearers. They seek to control the discourse by establishing themselves as enunciator and Jesus as enunciatee, not to be recipient of the word that becomes nourishing.

The enunciative context of DIS 3 is yet again different and stands out in contrast to the crowd's speaking (not a "true" discourse) immediately preceding. In vv 16–21 the discoursive partners are Jesus ("I") with his disciples, the silent "you" as implied by the you of "Do not be afraid" (6:20). Spatially both speakers are situated on the sea; temporally it is "after nightfall"; and the modality of Jesus' discourse is that of comforting the disciples. In this third discoursive exchange there is an immediate contrast in Jesus' refusal to respond to the crowd's acclamation and his response to the disciples' terrified silence (compare Mt 14:27; Mk 6:49). As enunciator ("I") Jesus has power and the disciples are both wordless and powerless as enunciatees to complete their trip. They may do so only *after and as a result of* Jesus' speaking. Like the disciples in DIS 1 who were empowered to complete their task of feeding the crowd as a result of Jesus' speaking ("Jesus gave thanks and distributed . . . "), the disciples in DIS 3 can finish their voyage as a result of Jesus' word ("he called out . . . and immediately the boat reached land"). Jesus' word has power.

DIS 4 is complex. It is made up of four parts; we shall take up the development of the discourse episode by episode. The discoursive partners are Jesus and the crowd. Except possibly for the second of the four exchanges (6:28-29), the crowd never assumes the proper enunciative role as "you" in relation to Jesus as "I." Throughout the discourse the crowd consistently occupies the enunciator's post as "I" in an attempt to control the discourse and Jesus. Spatially the location of the discourse is the Synagogue in Capernaum; temporally it is the "next morning," the day after the multiplication of bread and the crossing of the sea. The modus or intention of the crowd's discourse is to have Jesus provide "food" for them (6:25), but Jesus challenges their intention. The crowd does not appear interested in how Jesus came to this speaking location nor with expressing their real discoursive intention, their concern notwithstanding ("Rabbi . . . when did you come here?"). The true modus of the crowd's initial comment is exposed in 6:26—to have Jesus provide perishable food.

From Jesus' encounter with the crowd the power of his discernment is revealed. As he takes charge of the discourse (by assuming the enunciator's role) the inadequacy of their quest and their question to Jesus is combined with an improper identification of Jesus as King (6:14). The crowd still does not enjoy nor fully understand why they are not being nourished by Jesus: they are not looking for the right thing. Jesus now discloses the real object of their quest. It is not the food that gives life but the "perishable" food that they seek. Instead they should be seeking the "food that lasts, the food of eternal life," which the narrator shows comes through right discourse with Jesus, a right speaking/hearing relationship with Jesus.

In the second episode the crowd continues with another question, however the modus has now changed. The object of their search (perishable food) which Jesus has identified remains the same although their role in securing the food has changed: what are *they* to do to secure it? Again the impact of Jesus' previous words remains unfelt which means that they have not yet accepted the role of discoursive partner as defined and proposed by Jesus. Jesus' response is imperatival and the most forceful indicator of the control Jesus has as enunciator over against the enunciatee: believe in the one whom he has sent. He repeats in imperative form his previous imperative: "Work for the food that does not perish." Through his conversation with the crowd Jesus has begun to reveal the identity of the bread that does not perish and thereby to reveal the meaning of his original words by offering substitutional words, new words in place of old words.

At a third moment the crowd demands an example of a believable sign by ordering Jesus to "produce" for them. This time their "command" takes the form of a question which, it should be noted, carries with it an imperatival force. The basis for their demand is their interpretation of what the Scriptures, in particular the story of Moses and manna in the desert (Ex 16:14), says. As before Jesus refuses to respond to their order (he still remains the "he," the non-discursive partner, to their enunciation), and instead takes charge of the discourse (the "I") by correcting the crowd's understanding and discourse upon the text. Their problem is that they understand Scripture to the same degree that they understand Jesus' speaking!

First of all, it is not Moses who provided the bread in the desert but the Father who gave it then (*dedōken*) and gives it now (*didōsin*). Not only does Jesus correct the notion of who was subject of that action, he defines what the bread was in the past and what it is in the present. Indeed the Father continues to provide food as he did in the past. The difference is that the *present* food is imperishable. The shift in tense marks grammatically the shift in time and the shift in the nature of the "good" from past to present, manna in the past to that which comes through Jesus in the present. Indeed, the crowd does not realize it but by the time the discursive exchange is complete Jesus will have given them bread precisely *in and through his interpretation of the Scripture*. Jesus' discourse upon the Scriptures thus becomes the very sign that the crowd ought to be seeking but is incapable of understanding.

We can see this progression in redefinition and in the metaphorical equation of speaking-feeding in the following homology proposed by the crowd and completed by Jesus:

	PRESENT	PAST
CROWD	What sign? / You	Ancestors ate bread / "He" = Moses
JESUS	Jesus' Discourse / Jesus	Perishable food / "He" = the Father

In the fourth and final exchange in this discourse the crowd demands once again that Jesus provide the imperishable food in the same way that God provided perishable food in the past. Again, they speak as if they have not understood a word Jesus has said. Their continuing non-comprehension reveals their incapacity to engage in a discoursive relationship with Jesus. When they ask finally for bread in 6:30, thereby making explicit what was only implicit in 6:25, Jesus' response is to provide further self identification (6:20). Apparently his correction of the crowd's reading of Scripture and his metaphorical equation have gone unheard (non-you). The crowd's inability to read Scripture is matched by their inability to listen to what Jesus is saying to them, namely that he is bread of life and that his word is as life-sustaining for them as it was for the disciples on the sea ("It is I" = "I am the bread of life").

In the next discourse (DIS 5) the major enunciative change is a shift in the identification of the Jews as Jesus' enunciative partner. If the people have not made the connection between Jesus and the imperishable bread, the Jews all too clearly have. Along with a progressive identification of Jesus as the one who provides nourishment, indeed that it is his food that nourishes, another actor is now introduced into the narrative who, like the crowd, does not assume a proper discoursive relation with Jesus. This litany of disappointing discoursive encounters is an indicator within the narrative of the singular lack of success Jesus has had in finding a discoursive partner (recall that Philip and Andrew are in an acceptable relationship with Jesus in DIS 1). As was the case in Jesus' non-discourse with the crowd in DIS 2, there is again no discourse in the "conversation" with the Jews. The Jews only talk among themselves. Jesus is even less a discoursive "you"; he is reduced to the status of being a non-discoursive "he" (6:42) to be identified only obliquely through his words.

In one sense we could say that the discourse with the Jews ends before it begins, for in order to have enunciative relationship with Jesus the Jews have first to credit him with the status of a "you." At least with the people Jesus was provisionally cast in the role of an enunciatee (a "You") which he chose not to accept. By contrast, the Jews displace Jesus from their own discourse by their non-discoursive reference to him: Jesus is present to the discourse as a "he said" not as a "you." In particular this displacement takes place in the reference made to Jesus through his own words quoted by the Jews to one another ("I have come down from heaven," 6:42).

The discoursive similarity between the Jews and the people is underscored by the parallel scriptural misunderstanding (6:31) and the decontextualizing of Jesus' remarks. What is revealed in this parallel is a similar modus toward Jesus' words. What is different and ironic, however, is the Jews' *mouthing of Jesus' words* and their failure to recognize it for what it is as "food that lasts." In short, their incapacity to become discoursive partners and to eat the imperishable food is greater than the crowd's. The latter do not even recognize the importance of Jesus' words; the Jews do. They "eat" (speak) this imperishable food but cannot "stomach" it (cf. 6:60), just as the "many disciples" who similarly refuse to accept Jesus' words as life-giving and life-sustaining. In order to become a discoursive partner with Jesus one must do more than be spatially proximate to Jesus or even utter the very same words; a certain modus in the use of those words must prevail. A certain illocutionary force must be present. Being a discoursive partner with Jesus is a relationship that requires a continuing intentionality, for even former discoursive partners can betray Jesus (6:70-71).

Jesus responds to the Jews with an imperative and an instruction. By quoting Isaiah the prophet (Is 54:13) Jesus takes up an enunciative post and speaks Isaiah's words: "And they shall all be taught by God" (6:45). In the act of speaking Isaiah's words the enunciator Isaiah and the enunciator Jesus merge. The prophet's words are absorbed into Jesus' discourse in a way that contrasts with the distancing of Jesus as a discoursive partner and of his words on the part of the Jews. With this interpenetration of enunciative roles the authority of Scripture is attributed to Jesus' words which confirms why Jesus has been sought out in the first place—to come and listen and be taught—even if for certain hearers it is on their own terms. But it is plain from the murmuring of the Jews that they have not and are not listening either to Scripture or to Jesus' own words. Like the people they have not come to engage Jesus in discourse.

However, that is not the end of it. Jesus continues the defining process already begun with the disciples and the crowd. He is "the bread that comes down from heaven." Now that the Scriptures are taken up into Jesus' discourse they are given a new interpretative discoursive context. The result is a "true" understanding of what the bread is and what discourse with Jesus and Isaiah means: to come and listen to Jesus as a discoursive "you" is to (1) consume the bread of life and (2) to listen to the words of the prophet, which is to say the very words of God. Feasting on Jesus' words is consuming the word of God as spoken by Jesus.

In the second exchange of DIS 5 the Jews continue to speak to one another. This time, however, they do not utter Jesus' own words. Yet, they do not listen to what Jesus has to offer either—his word of (in both senses of origin and content) God. Jesus' power response ("in truth, in very truth I tell you . . .") is directed potentially to non-listeners and non-believers alike. In the absence of a communicative relationship Jesus nonetheless is going to establish some degree of communication. They have not heard the Scriptures from the start even though they possessed the Scriptures as a verbal sign and Jesus' word as an interpretant of that sign. Had they *listened* to him from the beginning they would have realized who and what Jesus was when he said "Where are we to buy bread to feed these people?" (6:5). Jesus is the imperishable food and the full disclosure and equation of Jesus with the bread is now complete.

In DIS 6 the spatial location remains the same (the synagogue in Capernaum). Temporally it is *after* Jesus' discourse with the Jews. The enunciative role of speaker has shifted now to "many of his disciples." Like the Jews before them, the modality of the disciples' comments is one of rejection and disbelief. Like the Jews before them the disciples speak to themselves; Jesus is distanciated from his communication. And Jesus is once again relegated to a non-discoursive role which he rejects (6:62) by assuming the enunciator's role and addressing a series of questions to them to which there is no reply. Jesus identifies his words as spirit (6:64), as life-sustaining (6:63). And just as the people and the Jews have come to Jesus for the wrong reason, so too many of his disciples have not really come to listen to him, or to hear the word of Isaiah and the word of God and to be nourished. For them as well his words are not easily "digestible" ("This is more than we can stomach! Why listen to such *talk*," 6:60). Rejecting Jesus' words is the same as saying that the good that lasts cannot be consumed! And if Jesus' words cannot be consumed then knowledge of God is not possible.

In DIS 7 the enunciative posts change once again. Now they are filled by Jesus and Simon Peter (for the Twelve). Temporally the discourse takes place "after that time," a reference to some unspecified time after the narrative events. Spatially there is no geographical reference, only an indication that the discourse is wherever Jesus is ("Lord to whom shall we go? Your words are words of eternal life," 6:68). The modality of Jesus' discourse is now that of testing. But in Simon Peter's response Jesus is identified appropriately as the Holy One of God, that is as a prophet (cf. II Kg. 4:9), as the place where the word is food. And this identification is done significantly in relation to Jesus as he *speaks*, with Jesus' words. It is proper now to identify Jesus in this way not because of what he does, though that is important, but by what he says. The discourse then ends with a question (6:70) for which there is no reply; it is addressed to a "you" which we can identify as the Twelve but also as an enunciatee who also may be the narratee of the text. This final question, as we will see, applies to the discoursive partners at the level of the narrated events and the narration. Quite appropriately then this final discourse brings the text to a conclusion at the narrated events level and opens it up for the narratee and implied reader of the text. For the latter two the conversation (or potential discourse) and identification of the discoursive partner for Jesus is only beginning.

C. NARRATIONAL LEVEL

The relation of mutual implication existing between the process of enunciation and the utterance is of importance in explaining the relation of the narrator's discourse to the narrative events and to the textual enunciation. The narrated events (the narrator's utterance which includes the actorial enunciation) of John 6 presupposes a narrational uttering (narrator's enunciation). In the same way, the narrational enunciation and utterance logically presuppose a textual enunciation with its textual enunciator (implied author) and textual enunciatee (implied reader). The identification of the narrator and narratee and of the narrational enunciation may prove difficult for the reason that a text may choose to hide the narrational enunciation within the narrative actions and speaking. While difficult, distinguishing between actorial and narrational enunciation is important in order to appreciate the various ways in which the narrational enunciation and its manifestation contribute to the overall textual effect. More difficult yet to determine and just as essential for an understanding of the text and its signifying power is the textual enunciation. For it is at the level of textual enunciation that one locates the fundamental *values* articulated in and through the narrational and narrative events.

Defining narrational discourse in enunciative terms is of great importance in giving a structural as opposed to historical description of the narrator's part in the text's meaning effect. In traditional exegetical terms the persona of the Evangelist is equated with the narrational enunciator and the Evangelist's audience with the narratee of the text. However, as we have suggested the discursive roles of narrator and narratee are to be viewed as textual *constructs*; they are intratextual realities to be fully distinguished from the flesh and blood persons responsible for the production and reception of the original written or oral text. Moreover, the narrator and narratee are as important a factor in the narrative unfolding of a text as the narrative actions themselves, for the narrational enunciation is responsible ultimately for the orchestration, development and interpretation of the events at the narrative enunciation level. By focusing upon the narrational roles in John 6 we can identify the way in which the narrational enunciator is responsible for directing the flow of narrated events in the discourse through a strategy of varying degrees of absence or presence within the text.

The narrator's presence/absence is discernible in a number of ways in John 6. Indices of the narrator's presence within the text not only mark a "speaking/hearing" role but also help signal a shift in the implied reader's movement from one level of the text to another. These "shifters" may in some instances take an overt, and in other instances covert, form. Overt shifters or enunciative markers when associated with the narrator help create a *distancing* effect between the narrator's speaking and the narrative events themselves. For example, "Some time later Jesus withdrew to the farther shore of the sea of Galilee (or Tiberias), and . . ." (6:1) signals a spatial distance as well as a temporal distance from Jesus' activities on the narrator's part. Temporal distance is communicated most readily with the use of demonstrative pronouns and the use of the aorist tense in narratives. For instance, the *tauta* of 6:1 refers backward in the text and in time to Jesus' miraculous and discoursive activity in Jerusalem in chapter 5. Markers of this sort thereby establish the time of the narrational speaking as coming at a time later than the narrative events.

The absence of overt markers of the narrator and the narratee's presence does not mean an absence of the narrational enunciation. Effacement of the narration (as illustrated in the "narrative" material in 6:16–21) is in fact a narrational technique for presenting the narrative events in a certain fashion, namely to create a stronger sense of objectivity and of truth. Such "realism" communicates the value of "true" and thereby shows the way in which the narratee's speaking modalizes or interprets the narrative world. In John 6 we find varying degrees of narrational presence and absence. Some of the more obvious ones are found in 6:41 ("At this time the Jews began to murmur disapprovingly because he said . . ."); 6:52 ("This led to a fierce dispute among the Jews"); 6:59 ("This was spoken in synagogue when Jesus was teaching in Capernaum"); and 6:66 ("From that time on . . .").

Another marker of the narrator's presence and the discoursive relationship with the narratee is the "explanatory" comment: 6:1 ("of Tiberias"), 6:4 ("The great Jewish festival"), 6:4 ("Jesus said . . ."); 6:6 ("This he said to test him; Jesus himself knew what he meant to do"); 6:22 ("Jesus, they knew, had not embarked with his disciples"); 6:64 ("For Jesus knew all along who were without faith and who was to betray him"); 6:71 ("He meant Judas . . ."). The function of these explanatory remarks is to inform the narratee of certain facts of the meaning of certain narrative events by letting the narratee in on the "true" nature of the narrative events. Explanatory comments communicate the truth value about events. For example, the narrator is privy to and communicates his knowledge of the intentions, attitudes, beliefs and motivations of the narrative actors in such a way as to signal the narrator's extraordinary knowledge and speaking authority.

In the case of John 6, these spatial, temporal, subjective and, importantly, modal indices point to the narrational enunciation. By identifying their character and the relationship of the narrator to the events within the narrative, we may be able to construct the character of the narratee in a similar way from the narrative events. In John 6 a progressive unfolding of the narrative events from the narrator's hand equips the narratee with a certain understanding of what the events are to mean. This developing understanding forms the narratee's enunciative role as it is constituted in the text. For the narratee in John 6 the progressive discoursive encounters at the level of the narrative events images the narratee's own development: the search for a more discoursive partner for

Jesus and the identification of Jesus is at the same time a search for and identification of a narratee who can appropriately be modeled as an effective listener. As Jesus' identity and his discoursive partner's identity are revealed through progressive encounter at the level of the narrative events, so the role of the narratee is formed in discourse with the narrator.

An important feature of the narration of John 6 is the shift that takes place between the past and the present and between narrative and discourse with the use of the aorist and historical present. Regular movement from one temporality to another accentuates the posterior status of the narrator/narratee discourse in relation to the narrative events: for example, in 6:25 ("they said" falls in the middle of a direct quotation) and 6:64b ("for Jesus knew. . . . So he said . . ." breaks apart one of Jesus' responses). At the same time the juxtaposition of narrative and direct quotation creates the effect of an interpenetration and modalization by narrational discourse of the discourse at the narrative events level. The use especially of the historical present helps to create a discoursive overlap, to establish multiple enunciative contexts because of the ambiguity of the enunciative indices along with the different enunciative levels of the text. The narratee and implied reader can thus enter into the text at varying levels as discoursive partners.

The first indication of the narrator's discoursive intent is found in the initial words of Jesus in DIS 1: "Where are *we* to buy bread to feed these people?" The inclusive personal pronoun "we" functions as an enunciative indice of the disciples and Jesus and also of the narrator and the narratee. Discoursive interpenetration makes this a question then at both discoursive levels. Moreover, the narrator's interpretative remark in 6:6 ("This he said to test him") draws the narratee's attention to the question and effectively signals the interpretative task ahead; this is a testing that perhaps will be of importance not only to the narrative figures but also to the narratee and implied reader as well. The stage is now set for both Jesus and the narrator to search through various discoursive contexts for an adequate *discoursive* partner and an adequate discoursive exchange. After the narrative presents Philip and Andrew, the people, the silent disciples, the people, the Jews, Jesus' many disciples and Simon Peter for the Twelve, the narratee is then in a position to judge which one of these discoursive exchanges with Jesus was an "adequate" or "true" discoursive model. This narrational process and the narratee's corresponding "growth in comprehension" are aspects of the performative action of the text, so that the work of the text is accomplished for the narratee and implied reader through the very act of entering the narrative events as discoursive partners.

The narrator's speaking directs the narratee toward a "right" selection of discoursive role. By presenting the narratee with a series of seven discoursive exchanges at the level of the narrative events, the narrator constructs a stance of point of view from which to evaluate and to select the appropriate discoursive role. In particular this choice requires the right modus or intention when engaging Jesus in discourse. But just how is one supposed to engage Jesus in discourse? To express doubt, to proclaim Jesus as King, to secure perishable food, to express doubt about Jesus' words or to express belief in Jesus and his words?

The narrator's point of view is aligned with Jesus' discoursive "I." When Jesus interacts with the various narrative personages the narrator does so as well (and by implication the narratee who takes on the "you" of the actors). At the narrative events level Jesus' discourse progressively identifies and then defines who the speaker, the "I," Jesus, really is. In DIS 1 Philip and Andrew are questioned about the source of bread for the crowd. Their response is off the mark because they have not discerned what is true but does not appear so about Jesus: namely that Jesus' words are food (6:63) and that what appears to be food is not. The narrator, however, is interested in doing more than merely equating "food" with "words"; the text does something more than engage in metaphorical elaboration of Jesus' words. The narrator in the text is in search iconically for a narratee who is able to answer Jesus properly, to engage Jesus in discourse. The search is on for a right narratee-listener and to use the narrative events as a template for that search.

That the search is underway is confirmed by the second discourse, or rather the lack of discourse! The people's affirmation of Jesus as King is met with Jesus' silence. The narratee's attention to this one-way conversation is further focused by the narrator who discloses the illocutionary force of the people's speaking ("they meant to come and seize him to proclaim him King," 6:15).

Jesus' words in DIS 3 are similarly unidirectional; however, the illocutionary force of Jesus' speaking is different from the discourse of the people in DIS 2. In 6:20 Jesus wants both to comfort the disciples and to provide a self-identification, an identification which gives further precision to Jesus' enigmatic bread statement in DIS 1. In contrast to the people's response, the disciple's behavior is more receptive. The juxtaposition of the disciples' silence and Jesus' silence in the preceding discourse points to the similarities and differences between Jesus and the disciples. Jesus refuses to respond out of power; the disciples refuse to speak out of weakness: the same behavior, different intentionality. With respect to the identification of Jesus in light of his multiplication of bread, Jesus is *not* prophet for what he does alone, but just as importantly for what he *says*. Failure to hold both word and deed together means failure to recognize Jesus' true identity. Just as important is an identification of Jesus' hearer. The narrator has begun to address this latter question by answering his *own* question in 6:5: Who, where is the bread? (6:20). Answer: "It is I," the one approaching the disciples walking and talking on the sea.

DIS 4 presents a four-stage discourse and another discoursive occasion in which "proper" discourse with Jesus is frustrated. First, far from being a discourse the exchange is merely a repetition of question and counter statement with no movement in the conversation. The crowd does not listen; it refuses to give up the enunciator's post to take on the "you" proposed by Jesus. Secondly, because the crowd does not listen it is unable to recognize food when it hears it. The narratee is led to evaluate this attempt at communication in a negative way. Finally, the juxtaposition of DIS 4 with a modestly successful hearing in DIS 3 parallels the semi-successful hearing that takes place in DIS 1 and DIS 2.

Like a conversation in which the parties never hear one another, the crowd asks a question to which Jesus gives a response that addresses another question. The tension in the communication enables the reader to see the incapacity of the crowd and the capability of Jesus. Jesus responds to the crowd's question but at a different level altogether. In the following chart are schematized the crowd's questions and Jesus' counter-responses:

CROWD'S QUESTION	JESUS' RESPONSE
When did you come here? (6:25)	You did not come for me but for bread (6:26)
What work do we do to obtain food? (6:28)	Believe in this bread (6:29)
What sign can you give? Moses gave bread. (6:30–31)	The Father, not Moses, gave it. He gives it now. (6:32)
Give us bread. (6:35)	Take it; here it is. (6:35)

In DIS 5 the narrator juxtaposes the "Jews" with the "crowd." As far as the narratee is concerned the enunciative subject of DIS 5 could be either the crowd or the Jews and later in DIS 6 even the crowd, the Jews or many disciples. The narrator presents the Jews also *as if* (apparently true, but actually not) in discourse with Jesus. However, the possibility of this conversation is made all the more remote by virtue of their speaking to one another and reducing Jesus to a non-discursive position. After giving an interpretation of the cause of the Jews' unrest (6:41), Jesus is seemingly identified (6:42) not in terms of what he did but of his family connections: they know his father and mother. Just as inept as the people, the Jews too do not understand. Yet in contrast with the crowd the Jews ironically mouth Jesus' own words and unknowingly (or knowingly?) possess the food which Jesus offers, imperishable food—his words—though this is not what they seek.

Jesus' response is to *teach*. He appeals to the Scriptures in a way that

(1) recalls the people's acclamation of Jesus as King (6:14) now explained in terms of teaching and (2) refers anaphorically to the crowd's mistaken interpretation of Moses, manna and the food that comes from God in the discourse immediately preceding. Jesus reinterprets metaphorically and thus expands the *egō eimi* of 6:20 and the *egō eimi ho artos tēs zōēs* of 6:35. In 6:45 the equation of coming and *eating* with coming and *listening* is affirmed. However the narrator does not abandon a gustatory code in favor of an auditory code; rather there is a broadening and developing of the gustatory identification of Jesus now to include the necessary auditory dimension: to *consume* Jesus' words is necessary to *listen* to his words, and in order to listen one must be a right hearer (unlike Philip and Andrew, the Crowd and the Jews). The identification of the speaker brings with it at the same time an identification of the listener.

At the level of narrative events the text moves progressively toward an identification of Jesus (by way of the Scriptures) as true food, i.e., as source of the prophetic word. At the same time there is a continuing deterioration in discoursive relations; while the true identity of Jesus becomes clear, the discoursive partners seem to become less and less capable. This is part of the narrator's strategy vis-a-vis the narratee: the greater the clarity regarding Jesus' identity the more pronounced the absence up through this point in the narrative of an adequate discoursive partner: as the enunciator Jesus ("I") comes into focus, the enunciatee ("you") flattens.

The progressive identification of Jesus for the narrator can be traced through the increasingly more specific *ego eimi* statements:
6:20   *egō eimi*
6:34   *egō eimi ho artos tēs zōēs*
6:51   *egō eimi ho artos ho zōn ho ek tou ouranou*
This progressive identification corresponds to a string of discoursive failures for the narratee:

PERSONAGE	DISCOURSIVE RELATION
Philip, Andrew	two-way, adequate
People	one-way, inadequate
Jews	one-way, inadequate
Many disciples	one-way, inadequate

The narrator's presence is marked forcefully again in 6:59. The narratee is immediately directed to the final discourse in temporal terms ("From that time on") through the chiastic movement of Jesus in discourse with the disciples, then with the crowd, the disciples, and then the Jews and finally back to discourse with the disciples. Discoursively the movement has proceeded from speaking in a certain fractured fashion to a refusal to listen and thus to communicate altogether (6:60), a movement from addressing Jesus as a discoursive partner at the beginning to reducing Jesus to a non-discoursive role at the end.

The narrator and narratee enter the narration in 6:66b with the question addressed to a plural "you" (*hymeis*) responded to by a singular Simon Peter (note that the plural "you" matches the plural "I" of 6:5). In addition the temporal deictic *ek toutou* creates the impression of a great temporal gulf between the narrational discourse and the narrated events. It is as if Jesus the actor has been distanciated from the abortive discourses in 6:1-65 and now returns to the Twelve-Simon Peter and speaks in an enunciative time contemporaneous with the narrational enunciation which effectively concludes the narrated events. Jesus' initial question in 6:8 is now finally answered: the *where* of the food (Jesus) and the *what* of the food (Jesus' words) are identified *pragmatically* in a proper kind of discoursive exchange with Jesus. For here in DIS 7 Simon Peter is presented as *the* disciple who accepts and properly fills the listening post vis-a-vis Jesus. If the strategy of the narrator is to identify an acceptable discoursive partner for Jesus, it is now revealed to be one-like-Simon Peter.

With the affirmation by Simon Peter and the use of the emphatic *hymeis* the narratee's association with Simon Peter is made enunciatively complete. However, the narrator is not finished; he gives the narration one final twist. Jesus identifies himself as the one who chooses the *hymeis* at the level of the narrative events (Simon Peter and the Twelve) and also in iconic fashion at the level of the narration (the narratee). On the one hand the testing procedure is complete when the narratee adopts Simon's own discourse and enters into Simon Peter's speaking as its "I." On the other hand the selection of a listener has already been made. Thus we could almost say that the discourse has programmed and chosen (or at least layed out the program for choosing) its own listener.

D. CREATING THE READER: THE TEXT'S WORK

It is at the third discoursive level (the textual enunciation) that we arrive at the intersecting point of the intra- and extra-textual domains. But before the text (which has been programmed to work in a certain way upon a scriptive reader) can work it has first to establish the enunciative roles of implied author and implied reader. In contrast to the scriptive author (the historical enunciator of the text) and the scriptive reader (the historical receiver of the text), the implied author is that structural principle which invests the textual world with its particular values, its semantic universe. Unlike the narrator or narratee who may have overt roles manifested within the text, the textual enunciator and enunciatee remain silent, constructed only indirectly and as a function of the whole text in relation to a scriptive hearer/reader.

Becoming the implied reader of a text and thus entering into discourse with the text means more than being the "you" for some speaking within the text; the implied reader is the one who accepts the value structure which the implied author proposes for the world of the text as reflected in and through the narrative events and the narration. Once this "perspective" or discoursive agreement is appropriated, the scriptive reader can enter into discourse with the text by assuming a particular role within the narrative or narrational events. It is in this way, then, that the text has the possibility of becoming a discoursive event. In Ricoeur's terms such a discoursive acceptance is necessary (an acceptance of both the enunciative post and the semantic universe which is presupposed) in order for the text "to be returned to discourse."

The work of John 6 at the textual enunciative level is not only the creation of the possibility of becoming a certain kind of partner in dialogue with Jesus or with the narrator; it is as well creation of a reader who comes "to believe" and "to understand" in a similar textual way. As such, the work of John's entire Gospel text calls for a careful description and deconstruction in order to situate the dimension of speaking/hearing which chapter 6 concentrates upon in relation to other actions which the textual enunciatee is brought to accept and to do. A comprehensive understanding of the textual enunciation therefore demands a reading of the whole Gospel text. In the absence of a full accounting of the textual enunciator and enunciatee roles we can only partially describe the world of values underlying the narration and the narrative actions forming the overall world of discourse which John's Gospel enunciates.

As a portion of that more extended reading, we can say that the work of John 6 as text is, in part, the performative act of creating a world in which the scriptive reader/hearer becomes a "you" for Jesus through the proffering of various models of narrative speaking and hearing. As an act of discourse, John 6 establishes a world of reference wherein the possibility of dialogue with Jesus is not only played upon through the success and failure of different discoursive partners within the text, but the *text itself* generates the possibility of re-creating that world outside of itself in relation to a scriptive reader/hearer, that dialogical relationship (both successful and not) with the scriptive hearer/reader himself/herself. In other words, the world *within* the text in which Jesus speaks by way of the narrator becomes a possible world *outside* of the text in which Jesus speaks by way of the text. In place of a figure Jesus (a narrative construct or interpretant) the reader only has the *text* of John 6 (also an interpretant within another signifying context).

Jesus' powerful and transforming word within the narrative is displaced at the textual enunciative level (though not at the expense, as was the case with the Jews and the disciples within the narrative, of communication with Jesus) by the words about Jesus' words. This transformation of one word into another word about that word is the very semiotic process whereby one sign generates a second from itself, and the second is a third, and so on ad infinitum. Peirce's perception of the perfusive nature of the sign is what allows us to explain the generative power of John 6 as text to create an "outside" world modeled iconically on and in response to the "inside" world of the text. And with that comes the possibility of a new scriptive reader/hearer in response to the presupposed textual enunciator/enunciatee of the text.

The distinctive character of John 6 is the use it makes of the narrative process of narrating Jesus' discourse as a way of demonstrating how one can engage or not engage Jesus in discourse, indeed the very possibility of having discourse with Jesus at all, a Jesus who is distanciated and displaced narratively by his own word. The text gives the implied reader, the narratee and the actors within the narrative the discoursive possibility of hearing, understanding and believing by providing enunciative markers of subject, time, place and modality for all to adopt. This play of the narrative upon becoming an "I" or "You" in relation to Jesus points to the play of the text in becoming the WORD (the narrator's word, Jesus' word, Isaiah's word and ultimately God's word) that sustains life.

It is John 6 as text which is the new locus of that narrative world and narrative Jesus speaking. It is John 6 as text with its power to create new worlds of discourse as a result of and in response to that narrative world in which the prophetic world is made equivalent to Scripture which is made equivalent to Jesus' word that continues to sustain and to produce new hearers for itself. John 6 is a text in search of its hearer in just that sense, a word looking for a place to happen, to be heard.

While John 6 combines gustative and auditive/enunciative codes metaphorically—which traditional exegesis points to as an indication of the Evangelist's *eucharistic* interests—the work of this text must not be reduced in a static way to what is uttered about Jesus in some constative identification of the themes contained inside the text. Rather, in keeping with what semioticians say about the generative power of language, and what Language Philosophy points to as the performative character of language, and what the narrative analysis indicates as a strategy for manipulation of the narratee, the word *about* Jesus is at the same time the word *of* Jesus; words about life in this sense are living words. John's text—Jesus' word—are in search of an ear to hear, a stomach that can digest, for whom the possibility exists for God to continue in the present of whatever reader/hearer to provide the imperishable food/word/story/text.

NOTES

/1/ Enunciation is defined for our purposes as the act of producing discourse. Depending upon whether one attempts to describe this aspect of language production from a semiotic perspective (A. J. Greimas) or from a language-use perspective (Oswald Ducrot), one can focus either upon the conditions that structure the act or the nature of the act's performative effect. For more see A. J. Greimas and Joseph Courtes, *Sémiotique: Dictionnaire raisonné du langage* (Paris: Seuil, 1979), s.v. "enonciation" (E. T. *Semiotics and Language: An Analytical Dictionary*. Trans. Larry Crist, Daniel Patte, Gary Phillips, *et al.* [Bloomington: Indiana University Press, 1982]). Oswald Ducrot, *Dire et ne pas dire: principes de sémantique linguistique*, Collection Savoir (Paris: Hermann, 1972), pp. 69–102.

/2/ C. Morris, *Signification and Significance: A Study of the Relation of Sign and Value* (Cambridge: MIT Press, 1964).

/3/ Chomsky is an excellent example of a linguist who privileges syntactics over both semantics and pragmatics.

/4/ This is a conflict represented most recently in the contrast between a saussurian dyadic view of sign versus a peircian triadic model. For a critique of the saussurian view, see J. Derrida, *Speech and Phenomena and Other Essays on Husserl's Theory of Signs*, trans. David Allison (Evanston: Northwestern University Press, 1973), p. 140.

/5/ See Ivan Almeida, "L'Opérativité sémantique des récits-paraboles. Sémantique narrative et textuelle. Herméneutique du discours religieux." Ph.D. dissertation. Université Catholique de Louvain, 1976, pp. 55–56.

/6/ Charles Sanders Peirce, *Collected Writings*, edited by Charles Hartshorne and Paul Weiss (Cambridge: Harvard University Press, 1934), 2.228.

/7/ See R. Bultmann, *The Gospel of John*, trans. G. R. Beasley-Murray, *et al.* (Philadelphia: Westminster, 1971), pp. 210–36; also compare Raymond Brown's segmentation in *The Gospel According to John*, Vol. 1 (New York: Doubleday, 1966), pp. 231–304.

/8/ See, for example, Daniel and Aline Patte, *Structural Exegesis. From Theory to Practice. Exegesis of Mark 15 and 16. Hermeneutical Implications* (Philadelphia: Fortress, 1978); and also Daniel Patte's *Paul's Faith and the Power of the Gospel: A Structural Introduction to the Pauline Letters* (Philadelphia: Fortress, 1983).

/9/ See Wolfgang Iser, "Narrative Strategies as a Means of Communication," in *Interpretation of Narrative*, edited by Mario Valdes and Owen Miller (Toronto: University of Toronto Press, 1979), pp. 110–17. Also see *Story and Discourse: Narrative Structure in Fiction and Film* (Ithaca: Cornell University Press, 1978).

/10/ See M. Tutescu, *Précis de sémantique française*, Etudes linguistiques, No. 19 (Paris: Klincksieck, 1975), p. 34.

/11/ The textual enunciator and enunciatee are to be distinguished from the actual producer (scriptive author, Gospel writer, etc.) and any speaking subject manifested within the text. In the terms of Julia Kristeva, the text's enunciator is the "subject of signifying praxis," a thoroughly *discoursive role* made possible by the interaction of a particular scriptive enunciator within her domain of discoursive practice, her speaking context. Similarly, the textual enunciatee is the subject *installed* within the text as its subject, one who is established by the *process* of the text's reading, a role generated out of the production of the text. See J. Kristeva, "The Subject in Signifying Practice," *Semiotexte* 1 (1975):19–26; S. Roudiez, "The Reader as Subject," *Semiotexte* 1 (1975):69–80.

/12/   Tutescu, *Précis de sémantique française*, p. 35.

/13/   See R. Jakobson, "Shifters, Verbal Categories and the Russian Verb," in *Selected Writings*, Vol. II *Word and Language*, (The Hague: Mouton, 1971), pp. 130–47; Emile Benvéniste, "L'Appareil formel de l'énonciation," *Langages* 17 (1970):14–19. Other terms used to designate the deictic function include: "expressive value" (Bally), "expressive function" (Buhler), "modes" (Empson), "egocentric particulars" (Russell), "token-reflexive expressions" (Reichenbach) and "indicator words" (Goodman).

/14/   See Richard Brecht, "Deixis in Embedded Structures," *Foundations of Language* 11 (1974):490; also see Charles Fillmore, "Deictic Categories in the Semantics of 'Come,'" *Foundations of Language* 2 (1966):219–27; and T. Todorov, "Meaning in Literature: A Survey," *Poetics* 1 (1971):9–10.

/15/   Benvéniste, "L'Appareil formel," p. 14.

/16/   See Ducrot, *Dire et ne pas dire*, pp. 221–47.

/17/   Emile Benvéniste, "Structure des relations de personne dans le verbe," in *Problèmes de linguistique générale*, Vol. 2, Bibliothèque des Idées (Paris: Gallimard, 1966), p. 195.

/18/   Greimas refers to this process in semiotic terms as "debrayage" or "disengagement." See *Dictionary*, s.v. "disengagement."

/19/   See D. Wunderlich, "Pragmatique, situation d'enonciation et deixis," *Langage* 26 (1972):49.

/20/   Compare Oswald Ducrot and T. Todorov, *Dictionnaire encyclopédique des sciences du language* (Paris: Seuil, 1972), s.v. "Temps."

/21/   Greimas refers to this phenomenon as "énonciation énoncé," which is part of the process of "engagement" ("embrayage") whereby the speaking subject installs self back into the time and space of the utterance; see *Dictionary*, s.v. "engagement."

/22/   Benvéniste, "L'Appareil formel," p. 15.

/23/   See W. J. Bronzwaer, *Tense in the Novel: An Investigation of Some of the Potentialities of Linguistic Criticism* (Groningen: Walter-Noordholl, 1970) and Kate Hamburger, *The Logic of Literature*, trans. Marilyn Rose, 2d. ed. (Bloomington: Indiana University Press, 1973), especially pp. 59–230.

/24/   Otto Jespersen, *Philosophy of Grammar* (London: Gallen and Unwin, 1924), p. 258.

/25/   See the full discussion of J. R. Frey, "The Historical Present in Narrative Literature, Particularly in Modern Germanic Fiction," *Journal of English and Germanic Philosophy* 45 (1946):52.

/26/   See F. Blass and R. Debrunner, *A Greek Grammar of the New Testament and Other Early Christian Literature*, trans. R. Funk (Chicago: University of Chicago Press, 1961), p. 32.

/27/   See Paul Ricoeur's discussion of "world" in "Interpretation Theory," (unpublished lectures delivered at the University of Chicago, 1971), p. 37.

/28/   See Charles Bally, *Linguistique générale et linguistique française*, rev. ed. (Berne: Francke, 1965), pp. 39–45.

/29/   Webster's *Third New International Dictionary*, s.v. "Modality."

/30/   Contemporary Language Philosophy following Austin and Searle directs attention in part to this aspect of language use with their categories of illocutionary and perlocutionary effects of language.

/31/   Tutescu, *Précis du sémantique française*, p. 18.

/32/   The specific criteria developed for segmenting the text into discoursive segments are (1) shift in discourse—when a new set of enunciative partners are engaged (for example, the change from Jesus speaking with Philip and Andrew to Jesus speaking with the crowd); (2) shift in speaking voice—a change in enunciator (for example, the movement from Jesus speaking to the narrator speaking); normally a change in enunciative partners indicates a discoursive change though not necessarily so; (3) narrating content and structure—shift from the speaking and doing context of one enunciator to another speaking and doing context (for example, the shift from the walk on water and discourse with the disciples to discourse with the crowd).

"NO NEED TO HAVE ANY ONE WRITE"?: A STRUCTURAL EXEGESIS OF 1 THESSALONIANS

Elizabeth Struthers Malbon
Virginia Polytechnic Institute and State University

Precis

This paper has both an exegetical and a theoretical goal. A structural exegesis of 1 Thessalonians, including an examination of both its syntagmatic structure and its paradigmatic structure, suggests a parallel between the "apostolic *parousia*" and the *parousia tou kuriou*: both aim to reestablish relationships, to fill an absence with a "presence." A typology of structural approaches to texts, based on a consideration of structuralist goals and textual foci, suggests both commonalities and distinctions among various structural approaches to texts and outlines a framework within which structural criticism might be said to operate.

I. INTRODUCTION

The problems of interpreting 1 Thessalonians are often approached historically. Commentators generally consider the date, place, and occasion of the writing of the letter and its situation in the context of Paul's ministry and travels, along with the authenticity, integrity, and unity of the letter. (Best; *IB* 11:245–53; *IDB* 4:621–25; *JBC* 2:227–28; Kummel: 255–62). Theological concerns are often, in effect, concerns for historical theology, e.g., *Paul's understanding* of the parousia. A more literary approach is taken by those interested in the epistolary "form" of 1 Thessalonians or of Paul's letters more generally (Funk, 1966:224–305; Funk, 1967:249–68; White; Doty). However, historical interest may dominate studies of the epistolary "form" as well, e.g., *Paul's adaptation* of first-century letter-writing conventions. Both historical studies and literary studies may seek to illustrate something identified as the "structure" of 1 Thessalonians; historical/theological studies may present an "outline of the content" (e.g., *IDB* 4:623–24; *IB* 11:251; *JBC* 2:228; Kummel: 255–56; Westermann: 120–21) while literary (epistolary) studies may present an "outline of the form" (e.g., Funk, 1966: 270; Doty: 43).

58   Semeia

Structural exegesis is literary rather than historical in orientation. Yet the present structural exegesis of 1 Thessalonians is not focused upon the text's "form" as a letter. It may perhaps be said that Funk's study is concerned with the "surface structure" of the text (as long as it is clear that a concern for "surface" structure is not a "superficial" concern!), while the present study seeks to investigate the "deep structure" or "depth structure" of the text (see Via, 1976:iii-iv). Keys to this investigation are the structuralist distinction between the syntagmatic and the paradigmatic dimensions of texts (or cultural phenomena)/1/ and Claude Lévi-Strauss's suggestion that repetition serves to make the structure of the text (or cultural phenomenon) apparent (443). Thus our procedure is to look for repeating elements in 1 Thessalonians as these make apparent the syntagmatic (or chronological) and paradigmatic (or "logical," theoretical) structure of the text. The search for such a "structure" is not dependent upon presuppositions about "the historical Paul" or first-century letter-writing conventions; it does, however, presuppose the potential meaningfulness of the text in the context of human communication. Our presentation is twofold: (1) a *structural exegesis of 1 Thessalonians*, including an examination of both its *syntagmatic structure* and its *paradigmatic structure*, and (2) a *typology of structural approaches to texts*, based on a consideration of structuralist *goals* and textual *foci*.

II. STRUCTURAL EXEGESIS OF I THESSALONIANS

A. SYNTAGMATIC STRUCTURE

A text may be delineated as an intricate web of syntagmatic and paradigmatic relations. Isolation of these two dimensions is possible only in the abstract. Simply stated, the syntagm is the chronological order of events, ideas, emotions, etc. presented in the text. The text of 1 Thessalonians as a whole, from 1:1 through 5:28, may be considered a single syntagm; however, repetitions within the text may suggest smaller syntagmatic units which clarify the structure of the text.

Even a quick reading of 1 Thessalonians/2/, and especially 1:2–2:16, brings to light the repetition of the phrase "you know": 1:5, "You know" (*kathōs oidate*); 2:1, "For you yourselves know" (*autoi gar oidate*); 2:2, "as you know" (*kathōs oidate*); 2:5, "as you know" (*kathōs oidate*); 2:11, "for you know" (*kathaper oidate*). To these five statements that "you know" is added one statement that "we know" (*eidotes*), 1:4. Comparable to assertions of "knowing" are assertions of "remembering": 1:3, "remembering" (*mnēmoneuontes*); 2:9, "For you remember" (*mnēmoneuete*). Variations on the simple expression of knowing or remembering are seen in 2:10, "You are witnesses" (*hymeis martyres*), and in 1:8, "we need not say anything" (*mē chreian echein hēmas lalein ti*). However, the observation that "we need not say anything" does not preclude the letter-writer's speech; the admission that the readers ("you") already "know" does not prevent the writer's recapitulation.

Statements which follow (or occasionally precede) an assertion of knowing (or remembering) often appear to be demonstrations or explanations of the fact of knowing; they are the evidence which supports the assertion. That Paul "give[s] thanks to God always" for the Thessalonians (1:2) demonstrates that Paul is "remembering" before God their "work of faith and labor of love and steadfastness of hope" (1:3). The coming of the gospel to the Thessalonians "not only in word, but also in power and in the Holy Spirit and with full conviction" (1:5) is explanatory of Paul's "knowledge" that God has chosen the Thessalonians (1:4)/3/. That the Thessalonians "know what kind of men" Paul and his colleagues "proved to be" (1:5) is demonstrated by the fact that the Thessalonians became "imitators of [them] and of the Lord" (1:6) and "an example to the believers in Macedonia and Achaia" (1:7). The fact that "the word of the Lord [has] sounded forth" from the Thessalonians and that their "faith in God has gone forth everywhere" (1:8a,b) explains why Paul feels no need to say anything (1:8c). The report that others make concerning the Thessalonians (1:9-10) demonstrates the aptness of Paul's perception. The Thessalonians' perceptions of Paul (2:1; 2:2a; 2:5a; 2:9a; 2:10; 2:11-12) are confirmed by Paul's recapitulation of his actions among them (2:2b; 2:5b; 2:6; 2:7a,b; 2:9b) and their response (2:13; 2:14-16). 2:13 portrays the Thessalonians' response as a positive demonstration that they "know" how Paul himself behaved (2:10) and how he "exhorted" them to behave (2:11-12); 2:14 offers a positive comparison between the response of the Thessalonians and that of the churches in Judea; 2:15-16 presents a negative comparison between the response of (the Judean Christians and) the Thessalonians and that of "the Jews."

At first glance, 2:3, 2:4, and 2:7c-8 might seem additional demonstrations or explanations of the Thessalonians' "knowledge" of Paul's ministry among them. However, these verses do differ from Paul's descriptions of his behavior and actions in 2:2b, 2:5b, 2:6, 2:7a,b, and 2:9b, which, although not narrowly specified, do indicate particular past actions in particular circumstances. 2:3-4a, on the other hand, reads more like the axiom underlying all such actions; it is an explanation asserted by Paul rather than a demonstration of explanation of something previously given as "known." Paul's conviction is that—negatively—"our appeal does not spring from error or uncleanness, nor is it made with guile" (2:3) and that—positively—"we have been approved by God to be entrusted with the gospel" (2:4a).

The implications of this conviction, implications for Paul's relationship with God and his relationship with the Thessalonians, are drawn out in 2:4b and 2:7c-8. This is our conviction (2:3-4a), Paul writes, "so we speak, not to please men, but to please God who tests our hearts" (2:4b). This is our situation, Paul explains, "so, having a strong affection for you, we take pleasure to share with you not only the gospel of God but also our own selves, because you have become beloved to us" (2:8, my own translation).

The above observations concerning 1:2–2:16 may be presented in the form of a chart of the type employed by Lévi-Strauss in "The Structural Study of Myth" (432–34). Repeated elements are listed below one another in vertical columns. Further attention to the relations between the columns is given below in considering the paradigmatic dimension of the text. The syntagmatic order of the text is followed by reading the chart from left to right and from top to bottom. Figure 1 illustrates our initial hypothesis: 1 Thessalonians 1:2–2:16 manifests a "structure" of four elements, which is made apparent by repetition in whole or in part—(1) assertion of knowing, (2) demonstration or explanation of knowing, (3) assertion of explanation or axiom, (4) implication(s) of assertion or axiom. The clearest expression of the fourfold pattern is given in 2:1–4 (which, according to Funk, is "formally" the opening of the body of the letter).

1	2	3	4
	1:2		
1:3			
1:4	1:5a		
1:5b	1:6		
	1:7		
	1:8a,b		
1:8c	1:9–10		
2:1			
2:2a	2:2b	2:3	
		2:4a	2:4b
2:5a	2:5b		
	2:6		
	2:7a,b		2:7c–8
2:9a	2:9b		
2:10			
2:11–12	2:13		
	2:14–16		

FIGURE 1

We must now consider whether such a "structure" is found elsewhere in 1 Thessalonians. 4:1–12 will provide the first test. The now familiar phrase "you know" does occur at 4:2 (*oidate gar*). (The reference to "know" in 4:4 [*eidenai*] appears to serve as a demonstration/explanation of that which "you know" in 4:2, more than as an additional assertion of something known. The reference to the "heathen" or "Gentiles" [*ta ethnē*] "who do not know God" at 4:5 is a negative transformation of a subjective, personal sense of "know" and will be discussed below.) More complex expressions indicating "knowing" are found at 4:1b, "as you learned from us" (*kathōs parelabete par' hēmon*), and at 4:9a, "you have no need to have any one write to you" (*ou chreian echete graphein humin*).

The demonstration that the Thessalonians learned from Paul (4:1b) is offered in 4:1a and c, which, in terms of the logic of the argument, follow 4:1b: you learned from us (4:1b); you are demonstrating that (4:1c); we "exhort you" (4:1a) to keep on doing so "more and more" (4:1c). 4:2 asserts that "you know what instructions we gave you through the Lord Jesus," and the instructions are reiterated (and thus this knowledge demonstrated and/or explained) in 4:3–6 under the heading "For this is the will of God, your sanctification" (4:3). That the Thessalonians were "forewarned" (4:6) by Paul explains, of course, how these various instructions (4:3–6) came to be "known" (4:2) by them. 4:7 is less a continuation of this list of particular injunctions and more a general principle underlying all such injunctions: "For God has not called us for uncleanness, but in holiness." This assertion justifies the instructions which have been explained (4:3–6) and are being demonstrated by the Thessalonians (4:1c). The implication of the assertion in 4:7 is made clear in 4:8, "Therefore whoever disregards this, disregards not man but God, who gives his Holy Spirit to you." The movement from 4:7 (note *akatharsia* and cf. *akatharsias* at 2:3, the only two occurrences of the term in 1 Thessalonians) to 4:8 parallels the movement from 2:3 to 2:4 (disregarding or rejecting not humanity but God at 4:8 and cf. pleasing not humanity but God at 2:4).

The fourfold pattern begins anew at 4:9a with the observation that "But concerning love of the brethren you have no need to have any one write to you. . . ." The basis for the Thessalonians' "knowledge" on this point is explained by the comment that they "have been taught by God (*theodidaktoi*) to love one another" 4:9b). The demonstration that this lesson is known is given in 4:10–11, "and indeed you do love all the brethren . . ." although, as in 4:1 above, "you" are "exhorted" to "do so more and more" (4:10). 4:12 brings out the implications of this love for the community, especially for its relationship to outsiders: "so that you may walk honorably among those outside and be dependent on no one" (my own translation). Thus the fourfold pattern uncovered in 1:2–2:16 also appears in 4:1–12 and may be charted as shown in figure 2.

1	2	3	4
	4:1a		
4:1b	4:1c		
4:2	4:3		
(4:4)	4:4–5		
	4:6	4:7	4:8
4:9a	4:9b		
	4:10		
	4:11		4:12

FIGURE 2

When we continue our reading of 1 Thessalonians against the background of this fourfold pattern, 4:13 comes as somewhat a surprise. Rather than an assertion of the Thessalonians' "knowing," 4:13 is an assertion of their "not knowing": "But we would not have you ignorant, brethren, concerning those who are asleep, that you may not grieve as others do who have no hope." Such a statement is a negative transformation, or an inversion, of the first element of the anticipated fourfold pattern. The second element, the demonstration/explanation of the asserted knowledge, is not to be expected if no knowledge has been asserted! Transformation of the situation of "ignorance" of the Thessalonians (4:13) demands some new word from Paul, and it is this which is introduced by 4:14 and elaborated in 4:15–17a. 4:14 is Paul's succinct statement of belief: "For since we believe that Jesus died and rose again, even so, through Jesus, God will bring with him those who have fallen asleep." This belief statement is an assertion on the order of those in 2:3–4a and 4:7; it is more an initial postulate than a resultant proof. 4:15,16, and 17a elaborate this belief in picturesque detail. The implications of this belief, which is offered (4:14–17a) as a counterpoint to the "ignorance" of the Thessalonians (4:13), are drawn out in 4:17b and 18. The first implication concerns the relationship of Paul and the Thessalonian Christians to "the Lord": "and so we shall always be with the Lord" (4:17b). The second implication concerns the internal relationships of the Thessalonian Christian community: "Therefore comfort (*parakaleite*) one another with these words" (4:18). Thus, although 4:13 inverts the expected opening, the fourfold pattern manifest in 1:2–2:16 and in 4:1–12 also appears in 4:13–18.

5:1–11 may be conceived, perhaps, as a doublet of 4:13–18. A double assertion of "knowing" is presented in 5:1 and 2—"you have no need to have anything written to you" (*ou chreian echete humin graphesthai*, 5:1) and "For you yourselves know well" (*autoi gar akribos oidate*, 5:2). The "knowledge" which is asserted is the manner in which "the day of the Lord" will come, and it is this "knowledge" which is demonstrated/explained in 5:3. The entire section, 5:2–8, moves forward by a play on the eschatological term "day of the Lord"—day *vs.* night, light *vs.* darkness. "But you are not in darkness, brethren" (*hymeis de, adelphoi, ouk este en skotei*, 5:4) is yet another assertion of "knowing," and 5:5 and 5:7 an additional (and metaphorical) demonstration/explanation of what is presented as "known." 5:6 (note *ara oun*) and 5:8 present implications, again metaphorically expressed, of such "knowledge" and should be compared with 2:4b, 2:7c–8, and 4:12. The axiom underlying this knowledge (5:1,2,4) as demonstrated/explained (5:3,5,7) is boldly stated in 5:9–10a: "For God has not destined us for wrath, but to obtain salvation through our Lord Jesus Christ (5:9), who died for us (5:10a). . . ." As in 4:17b–18 above, the implications of the asserted belief (4:14–17a; 5:9–10a) are twofold, involving the relationship of Christians to the Lord (5:10b, "so that whether we wake or sleep we might live with him") and the relationships of Christians among themselves (5:11a, "Therefore encourage [*parakaleite*] one another and build one another up . . .").

Both 4:13–18 and 5:1–11 direct the Thessalonians toward an assured and constant relationship with the Lord and a supportive relationship with each other. 4:13 opens this section with an assertion of "ignorance" on the part of the Thessalonians, but 5:11b closes this section with a demonstration of their "knowledge": "just as you are doing" (*kathōs kai poiete*); compare *kathōs kai peripateite* at 4:1, the opening of the larger section, chapters 4–5. These observations on 4:13–5:11 may be charted as were those on 1:2–2:16 and 4:1–12.

1	2	3	4
4:13 (-)			
		4:14	
		4:15	
		4:16	
		4:17a	4:17b
			4:18
5:1			
5:2	5:3		
5:4	5:5		5:6
	5:7		5:8
		5:9–10a	5:10b
			5:11a
	5:11b		

FIGURE 3

We turn now to 2:17–3:10, the section of 1 Thessalonians generally labeled "the travelogue." But our precedure calls for considering this section without this prior label and in the same manner in which we have evaluated the other portions of the text. We wish to determine whether or not the fourfold pattern discovered elsewhere in 1 Thessalonians appears at 2:17–3:10 as well. The section is indeed complex, but our analysis of 4:13–5:11 offers several clues for understanding 2:17–3:10. Near the close of the section, 3:7, with its use of *paraklēthēmen*, seems to parallel 4:18 and 5:11a. At the opening of the section, 2:17a seems to parallel 4:13 as an assertion not of "knowledge" but of "ignorance."

Paul's experience of the spatial and temporal distance between himself and the Thessalonian Christian community seems to be felt as a situation of "not knowing," as 2:17a suggests and 3:5b,c makes plain: "that I might know your faith, for fear that somehow the tempter had tempted you and that our labor would be in vain." 2:17b–18 demonstrates/explains why Paul has "no knowledge": he has been "hindered" from visiting the Thessalonians, even though he has desired to visit them "again and again." The rhetorical question at 2:19 and the strong statement at 2:20 function as the underlying motivation for Paul's desire to visit (2:17b–18), the axiom behind the action: "For what is our hope or joy or crown of boasting before our Lord Jesus at his coming? Is it not you? (2:19) For you are our glory and joy (2:20)." The action resulting from this assertion (2:19–20) is, not surprisingly, a renewed attempt on Paul's part to make contact with the Thessalonians. The failure of a proposed personal visit (2:17b–18) has left the status of "no knowledge" unchanged (2:17a); thus a visit by an intermediary is proposed (3:1–3a; 3:5a) to transform Paul's "not knowing" to "knowing" (3:5b,c): "Therefore when we could bear it no longer (3:1; cf. 3:5a), . . . we sent Timothy, our brother . . . (3:2), . . . that I might know your faith (3:5b)." The thrust of Paul's argument at this point is, perhaps, more clear than the order and manner of its presentation, which manifests not only intellectual reasoning but also emotional response.

1	2	3	4
Paul does not know how the Thessalonians are faring,	for he has been hindered in his desire to visit them.	But the Thessalonians are Paul's glory and joy,	so he sends Timothy to them on his behalf, to inquire and exhort.

The transforming result of Timothy's visit to the Thessalonians and return to Paul (Paul's lack of "knowledge" of the Thessalonians' faith ⟶ Paul's "knowledge" of the Thessalonians' faith) is reported at 3:6, but it is foreshadowed at 3:3b, 3:4a, 3:4b by the statement of the Thessalonians' "knowledge" of Paul's ministry. It is *as if* Paul, who had worried that the Thessalonians might "be moved by these afflictions" (3:3a), is so excited by Timothy's "good news" of their faith and love (3:6a) that he cannot restrain himself to recount his response in the proper chronological order; at the mention of "these afflictions," Paul's tribute to the Thessalonians' "knowledge" of himself and his ministry spills out. A double assertion of "knowledge" (3:3b, "You yourselves know," *autoi gar oidate*; 3:4b, "just as it has come to pass, and as you know," *kathōs kai egeneto kai oidate*) frames a demonstration/explanation of this "knowledge" (3:4a). The "good news" of Timothy reestablishes Paul's "knowledge" of the Thessalonians (3:6a) as Paul learns that the Thessalonians have not failed in their "knowledge" of him: "that you always remember us kindly and long to see us, as we long to see you . . .(3:6b)."

The implication of this renewed "knowledge" for Paul's relationship with the Thessalonian Christian community is drawn out in 3:7, "for this reason, brethren, in all our distress and affliction we have been comforted (*paraklēthēmen*) about you through your faith. . . ." Like 4:13-18, 2:17-3:10 opens with an inversion, or negative transformation, of the first element of the anticipated fourfold pattern, yet manifests the pattern in a recognizable and basically positive way, moving toward *paraklēsis* (consolation, exhortation) as the implied action. 3:8 and 9, paralleling 2:19 and 20 in reverse order, present a strong statement (3:8) and a rhetorical question (3:9) which assert that the Thessalonians are Paul's joy. This assertion motivates the movement from absence and "not knowing" to Timothy's visit and report and "knowing." 3:10, Paul's constant prayer for the Thessalonians, demonstrates that his "knowledge" of the Thessalonians has indeed been renewed. While 3:8-9 parallels 2:19-20, 3:9-10 parallels 1:2-3. Prayer (1:2, *proseuchōn*; 3:10, *deomenoi*) and thanksgiving (1:2, *eucharistoumen*; 3:9, *eucharistai*) frame the first half of Paul's letter to the Thessalonians. These observations of 2:17-3:10 may be charted in the previously established manner. Additional markings indicate certain internal relations of 2:17-3:10, as discussed above.

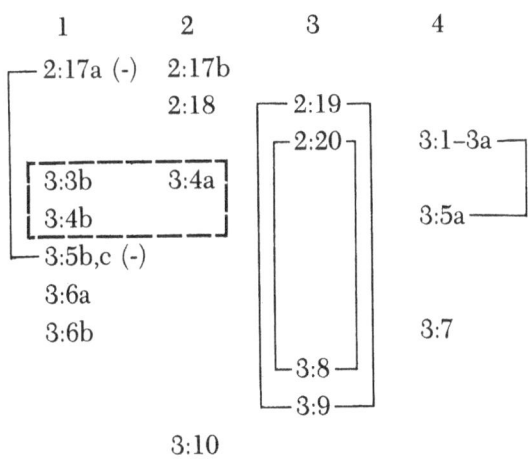

FIGURE 4

Thus we have illustrated the presence of a fourfold pattern in 1 Thessalonians 1:2–2:16, 2:17–3:10, 4:1–12, and 4:13–5:11. This "structure," presented above basically in its syntagmatic dimension, was discovered by following Lévi-Strauss's suggestion that "repetition has as its function to make the structure of the myth apparent" (443). Divisions suggested by the historical or theological "content" of the letter or by the *epistolary* "form" of the text have been overlooked in this search for what may be termed the *mythic* structure. This mythic structure will be considered in its paradigmatic dimension below, but first we must consider several groups of verses of 1 Thessalonians which remain to be evaluated: 1:1, 3:11–13, 5:12–22, 5:23–24, 5:25–28.

The fourfold pattern which was found to be repeated throughout 1:2–2:16, 2:17–3:10, 4:1–12, and 4:13–5:11 does not appear to extend to 1:1, 3:11–13, 5:12–22, 5:23–24, and 5:25–28. In the former passages a mythic structure appears to leave a heavy impress on the letter, while in the latter passages the marks of an epistolary structure appear dominant.

1:1 is the salutation of the letter, consisting of sender (1:1a), addressee (1:1b), and greetings (1:1c). Traditional commentators are not in strict agreement concerning the extent of the formal closing of 1 Thessalonians. At the very least, 5:28 is listed; 5:28 parallels 1:1c, the initial greeting. However, it is difficult to categorize 5:25,26, and 27 other than as greetings as well, in which case 5:25–28 parallels 1:1. 3:11–13 is a prayer, a blessing, which closes the first half of the letter; 3:11–13 is paralleled by 5:23–24, a blessing which closes the second half of the letter. As the first half of the letter is dominated by thanksgiving (note the framing references to "giving thanks" in 1:2–3 and 3:9–10, as well as the additional reference in 2:13 and the overall tone), a blessing forms an appropriate conclusion. The second half of the letter is dominated, however, by exhortation (note the framing references to "exhorting" in 4:1 and 5:11, additional references in 4:10 and 4:18, and the overall tone, but also the exhortation [5:14] to "give thanks in all circumstances" [5:18])/4/, and, it would appear, an exhortation (5:12–22) and a blessing (5:23–24) together form the conclusion. Thus:

1:1	greeting
1:2–3:10	(thanksgiving)
3:11–13	blessing
4:1–5:11	(exhortation)
5:12–22, 23–24	exhortation, blessing
5:25–28	greeting

Although 1:1 and 5:25–28 and 3:11–13 and 5:12–22, 23–24 do not manifest the same "structure" uncovered in the larger intervening passages (1:2–3:10; 4:1–5:11), certain emphases are common to both groups.

Everywhere a system of relationships among "persons" is of importance: Paul relates to the Thessalonians (see especially 1:1; 3:11–12; 5:25–28; cf. especially 2:8; 2:19–20; 3:8–9), God and/or the Lord and/or the Holy Spirit relate/s to the Thessalonians or all Christians (see especially 1:1b; 3:13; 5:16–18; 5:19–20; 5:23–24; 5:28; cf. especially 4:7–8; 4:14; 4:17b; 5:9–10), God relates to Paul (see especially 3:11; cf. especially 2:3–4), the Thessalonians relate to each other (see especially 3:12; 5:12–15; 5:26; cf. especially 4:12; 4:18; 5:11a).

1 Thessalonians is often cut lengthwise, as it were, into two halves: chapters 1–3 and chapters 4–5. 1 Thessalonians may also be cut crosswise, again as it were, into two groups: portions in which an epistolary structure is dominant (1:1 // 5:25–28; 3:11–13 // 5:12–22, 23–24) and portions in which a mythic structure is dominant (1:2–2:16 // 4:1–12; 2:17–3:10 // 4:13–5:11), although both an epistolary and a mythic structure may be assumed to be operative at some level throughout.

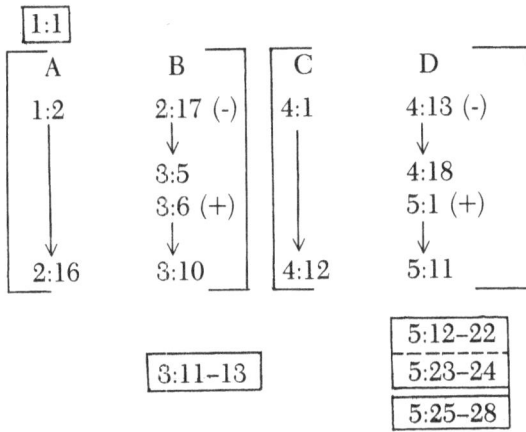

FIGURE 5

A graphic outline which reflects the observations made of 1 Thessalonians to this point is presented in figure 5. The various parts and sections of the text are interwoven in a number of ways. 1:1 and 5:25–28 frame the text as a letter; 3:11–13 and 5:12–22,23–24 close its two halves. The major portions of the text may be divided into four groups based on the way each group manifests the mythic structure (the fourfold pattern): in groups B and D the initial manifestation of the first element of the fourfold pattern is an inversion (-), although the pattern later appears with the first element as anticipated (+). 1:2–3 and 3:9–10 (note "give thanks," "thanksgiving") enclose 1:2–3:10 (A and B), as 4:1 and 5:11 (note "exhort") enclose 4:1–5:11 (C and D). References to holiness and pleasing God (2:3–4; 4:7–8) interrelate group A (1:2–2:16) and group C (4:1–12), while references to exhorting one another (3:7;

4:18; 5:11a) interrelate group B (2:17–3:10) and group D (4:13–5:11). Holiness and exhortation (and comfort—both *paraklēsis* in Greek) appear to epitomize divine-human and human-human relationships respectively; the blessing at 3:11–13 and the exhortation/blessing at 5:12–22/23–24 crystallize this view. Paul's personal relationship to the Thessalonians is critical throughout, as signaled by the beginning (1:1) and the end (5:25–28).

Figure 5 reflects both epistolary and mythic structures, both syntagmatic and paradigmatic dimensions. The mythic structure is of greater concern in the present analysis, but in those passages enclosed by rectangles the epistolary structure is considered dominant. Following the arrows and the consecutive numbers of the passages themselves illustrates the syntagmatic dimension. However, the division of the passages into groups (columns) A, B, C, and D is made in consideration of the paradigmatic dimension as well.

Figures 1 through 4 may be read syntagmatically by reading the horizontal rows from left to right and from top to bottom. Figures 1 through 4 may be read paradigmatically by ignoring the horizontal rows and reading the vertical columns from left to right, each column being considered as a unit (cf. Lévi-Strauss: 433). Our attention now turns to this paradigmatic reading.

B. PARADIGMATIC STRUCTURE

According to Lévi-Strauss, the syntagmatic dimension of a myth presents only its "apparent content," whereas the paradigmatic dimension reveals its "latent content." However, an actual text is formed of interwoven syntagmatic and paradigmatic strands, and the two are fully unraveled only at the risk of destroying the fabric of the text. Analytically, though, the paradigm may be isolated as the "logical," theoretical structure of the text, and, in Lévi-Strauss's view, the mediation of opposites is key to the mythic paradigm.

The verses indicated in figures 1–4 are arranged in columns on the basis of repeating elements, and these elements may be considered basically as actions. Central to the verses listed in column 1 is an assertion of knowing or an assertion of knowledge. The focus of the verses in column 2 is the enactment of a demonstration or explanation (of the knowledge or "non-knowledge" asserted in column 1). Column 3 is comprised of passages which make an assertion which itself may be an underlying explanation. The passages in column 4 suggest action or actions which follow from previous assertions (generally of column 3), that is, implications. In analyzing the Oedipus myth and certain Zuni myths, Lévi-Strauss found that the four columns which emerged could be related as follows:

$$1 : 2 \; :: \; 3 : 4$$

that is, 1 is to 2 as 3 is to 4. My analysis of 1 Thessalonians 1:2–3:10 and 4:1–5:11 may also be depicted in this form.

This pattern of relations is expressed in a more complex form in Lévi-Strauss's formula for the structure of myth:

$$fx(a) \; : \; fy(b) \; :: \; fx(b) \; : \; fa\text{-}1(y)$$

where "x" is opposed by "y," and "a" is opposed in one way by "b" and in another way by its own inverse, "a-1." In addition, in the fourth and final element of the formula, function and term values are reversed: "y," which had appeared as a function, now appears as a term; "a" had appeared as a term and now the "inverse of a" appears as a function. This final element of the formula indicates the mediating and transforming power of myth, the power of myth to move beyond its starting point in the manner of a spiral/5/. The formula may be applied to 1 Thessalonians as illustrated in figure 6. At this level of abstraction, the formula may seem but a play with words, but a return to the text (using figures 1–4 as guides) embodies the abstract terms with narrative significance. For example:

1	2	3	4
The Thessalonians know Paul's exemplary ministry and the instructions of the Lord,	as demonstrated in their exemplary behavior.	For holiness before God and mutual exhortation are required of Christians,	and these lead to holistic relationships with both God and other people.

terms: a	= (Objective) Knowledge	
b	= Demonstration/Explanation	
a-1	= (Subjective) Knowledge	
y	= Action	
functions:	fx	= asserted
	fy	= enacted
	fa-1	= (subjective) knowing

fx(a)	:	fy(b)	::	fx(b)	:	fa-1(y)
asserted		enacted		asserted		(subjective)
(Objective)	:	Demonstration/	::	Explanation/	:	knowing
Knowledge		Explanation		Demonstration		Action

FIGURE 6

Lévi-Strauss's formula for the structure of myth is concerned with the relationship between relationships. In terms of 1 Thessalonians this means that the relationship of asserted (Objective) Knowledge to enacted Demonstration/Explanation is comparable to the relationship of asserted Explanation/Demonstration to (subjective) knowing Action. As enacted Demonstration/Explanation completes or fulfills asserted (Objective) Knowledge, so (subjective) knowing Action completes or fulfills asserted Explanation/Demonstration. Furthermore, as the second element fulfills or extends the first, and the fourth fulfills or extends the third, so the third and the fourth move beyond the first and the second, giving to the whole movement a heliodoidal shape. 1 Thessalonians aims toward the reestablishment of relationships: human–human (especially Paul–Thessalonians) and human–divine (especially Thessalonians [living or dead]–the Lord). Such reestablishment of relationships is a (subjective) knowing Action.

The difference between objective knowledge, i.e., knowing a fact, and subjective knowledge, i.e., knowing a person, is the difference between knowing instructions and knowing God and fellow Christians. Of the thirteen occurrences of *oida* in 1 Thessalonians, all but two are statements of knowing that (or knowing *how*, 4:4), even though *knowing that Paul* acted in such-and-such a way (1:5b; 2:1,5,11–12; 3:3b,4; 4:2) or *knowing that God* acts in such a way (1:4; 3:4?; 5:2) is usually signified/6/. However, at 4:5 the people (*ta ethnē*) "who do not know God" are contrasted with the Thessalonians who, thus, must "know God"—personally, subjectively, that is, as subject to subject. At 5:12, part of the final exhortation, Paul encourages the Thessalonians "to know [*eidenai*, perfect infinitive of *oida*, translated 'to respect' by RSV] those who labor among you and are over you in the Lord and admonish you. . . ." This too signifies a subject to subject knowing. Both God and fellow Christians are to be known in this personal, subjective way—not just known about. Knowing *about* or knowing *that* is not detrimental—indeed, it is essential; but it is partial. Paul's statements that the Thessalonians have no need to have any one write to them "concerning love of the brethren" (4:9) or "as to the times and the seasons" of the day of the Lord (5:1) are assertions that more (Objective) Knowledge is not needed. However, the very writing of Paul's letter to the Thessalonians suggests another need: the need for (subjective) knowing Action, i.e., the need to express and strengthen the personal knowing of one another and of God (and the Lord) in action, including the action of letter-writing!

It is this need which Robert Funk has considered from another angle in examining the "apostolic *parousia*" in the Pauline letters. Funk's thesis is as follows: "Owing to Paul's understanding of the significance of his apostolic presence to his congregations, Paul gathers the items which may be scattered about in the common letter or appended as additional information, into one more or less discrete section, in which he (a) implies that the letter is an anticipatory surrogate for his presence, with which, however, the letter is entirely congruent (2 Cor. 10:11); (b) commends the emissary who is to represent him in the meantime; and (c) speaks of an impending visit or a visit for which he prays. Through these media his apostolic authority and power are made effective" (Funk, 1967:266).

However, as Funk suggests in two footnotes, in 1 Thessalonians the real focus of the relevant section (2:17–3:13) is "the Pauline notion of the reciprocal presence of apostle and congregation to each other" (Funk, 1967:251, n. 1, cf. 266, n. 1; see 1 Thessalonians 3:6–8; cf. 2:19f.). I judge that in 1 Thessalonians *greater* weight is given to the significance of the "presence" of the congregation to the apostle. The Thessalonians may have "no need to have any one write," but Paul has a great need to write!

In this sense, the act of Paul in writing to the Thessalonians (after hearing from them via Timothy) is more important than the "facts" the letter contains; the letter is more something done than something said. A letter as letter presupposes a relationship between sender and receiver/7/; to the extent that expressing and solidifying this relationship is more important than whatever "news" may be conveyed, a letter is a "performative" text. In 1 Thessalonians, this assumption of the letter as letter is also manifest in the mythic structure of the letter: one form of (subjective) knowing Action is the writing of letters.

Funk's concern is the "form and significance" of the Pauline letter, especially the "apostolic *parousia*" (of which the so-called "travelogue" is one aspect); 1 Thessalonians 2:17–3:13 serves as one example. My main concern is the mythic structure of 1 Thessalonians as a whole, and in this approach 2:17–3:10 is to be understood in its context within 1 Thessalonians. Within this context, a parallel between 2:17–3:10 and 4:13–5:11 is suggested. It is *as if* Paul answers the questions and comforts the anxieties of the Thessalonians concerning the absence of those who have died on the basis of his own experience of questions and anxieties brought about by his absence from the Thessalonians. As Timothy's "good news" of the Thessalonians' faith and love comforts Paul (3:6–7), so Paul's "word of the Lord" concerning the resurrection of the dead is intended for the comfort of the Thessalonians (4:14–18). As Paul's relationship with the Thessalonians proves to be secure despite his absence from them, so the relationship of living and dead Thessalonian Christians is secure despite their absence from one another. Both the "apostolic *parousia*" and the *parousia tou kyriou* aim to reestablish relationships; both intend to fill an absence with a "presence." The structure of the letter as letter (Funk's analysis) does not suggest this parallel; it is suggested by the mythic structure of the text.

The mythic structure of 1 Thessalonians 1:2–3:10 and 4:1–5:11 has been analyzed syntagmatically as a repeating series of actions of four types: 1, 2, 3, 4. The mythic structure of 1 Thessalonians 1:2–3:10 and 4:1–5:11

has been analyzed paradigmatically as the interrelation of the four types of actions: 1 : 2 :: 3 : 4. Basically, these analyses have followed the procedure of Lévi-Strauss in "The Structural Study of Myth"/8/.

III. TYPOLOGY OF STRUCTURAL APPROACHES TO TEXTS

The conclusions of the present structural exegesis of 1 Thessalonians repeat neither the outline of the "content" nor the outline of the "form" generally presented by commentators, although, in certain aspects, the "structure" proposed herein may be compared with both "outlines." Traditional criticism is historically oriented in outlining the "content" of biblical texts; e.g., 1 Thessalonians is viewed as a source of information about Paul's ministry. Structural criticism is literary in orientation and often focuses not on the "surface" of a text (e.g., the "form" of a narrative as a narrative or the "form" of a letter as a letter) but on the "depth" dimension of a text (in Lévi-Straussian terminology, the mythic dimension) or on the relationship between "surface" and "depth." Thus it is perhaps over-simplified and yet helpful to characterize traditional criticism as historical and structural criticism as literary (Via, 1975:72), traditional criticism as diachronic and structural criticism as synchronic (Patte, 1976:9–20; Via, 1975:1–7; McKnight, 239–48; Polzin, 9, 17–18, 201), traditional criticism as focused on the "author" and structural criticism as focused on the "text" (Culley: 166–71).

Yet, "structural criticism" (like "traditional criticism") while singular grammatically, is plural in manifestation! It is not our purpose here to define "structuralism," nor to describe "structural exegesis" in all its varied manifestations. Our aim is, rather, to consider briefly what is common to a variety of endeavors identified as "structural" or "structuralist"/9/ and what distinguishes them, and to set within this framework the present study of 1 Thessalonians. This approach to "structuralism" and "structural exegesis" concentrates on end points and beginning points, *goals* and *foci*. The following theoretical construct or typology was originally developed in relation to narrative texts and is here expanded to include letters ("epistolary texts") and to illustrate certain commonalities between the two.

A. GOALS

Because of divergent intentions, methods, and results of thought and works labeled by their authors or by others as structural or structuraist, it is not easy, perhaps not possible, to complete the statement, "structuralism is . . ." I should like, instead, to present several alternatives to the statement, "structuralism as . . ." In other words, while agreeing in principle with those who find structuralism impossible, or nearly so, to *define*, in practice I have found it helpful to systematize several important goals of structuralism's "adherents" or "practitioners."

I employ the two terms "adherents" and "practitioners" advisedly, for structuralism in its broadest sense may aim toward either ideology or methodology. These two basic directions are not unique to structuralism, but common to intellectual movements generally; they represent what Michael Lane (13) refers to, although with somewhat different labels, as the two categories of "the means that men employ to order their universe"/10/. By ideology—or philosophy if its connotations are less abrasive/11/—is meant "any more or less consistent system of beliefs and values which describes and accounts for the relations of men to one another, and to the material, and not infrequently the immaterial, universe" (Lane: 13/12/). Structuralism as an ideology is "a way of looking for reality not in individual things but in the relationships among them" (Scholes: 4). Lévi-Strauss's desire to understand the structure of the human mind from an examination of its cultural products, his discovery of "vast homologies" (Bovon: 11), represents an ideological (or philosophical) goal of structuralism. By methodology is meant "any set of rules or regulations which describes and prescribes the operations to be performed upon any matter . . . with the purpose of ordering it and understanding its working" (Lane: 13). Most structuralists view structuralism as a methodology, although they may recognize that its basic presuppositions are philosophical. I offer this distinction between ideology and methodology as a descriptive one/13/ not as an evaluative one, although "ideology," or its equivalent, generally serves as the negatively valued pole among commentators on structuralism. In fact, neither ideology nor methodology is manifest concretely in total isolation—in structuralism or in any intellectual movement (Lane: 13).

But, speaking abstractly, structuralism as a methodology may focus upon either theory or analysis/14/. Structuralism as theory may be directed to various issues: a theory of Russian fairy tales (Propp), a theory of kinship or myth (Lévi-Strauss), a theory of narrativity (Greimas). In the field of literature, theoretical structuralism approaches not so much the meaning of individual works of literature as the meaning of meaning, that is, the presuppositions which enable literature to be written and to be read; theoretical structuralism seeks not so much to tell the meaning as to recreate the process of meaning. From this description, the reverberations between theory and ideology should be loud and clear; in somewhat simplistic terms, ideology may be understood as theory (or theories) further abstracted and further generalized.

In the other direction, theory is resonant with analysis, for analysis is applied theory. In the field of literature, structuralism as analysis focuses upon the meaning of individual works, although this meaning must be considered (theoretically) as a subset of the meaning of meaning. Structuralism as analysis is concerned not just with the *what* of individual meaning, but with the *how* of individual meaning. Observers have often noted that structuralism as theory appears dominant over structuralism as analysis; some commentators have even identified structuralism as theory with "structuralism" *per se*. Since theoretical hypotheses offer starting points for analysis, theoretical dominance may be a mark of structuralism's youth; if so, signs of maturation (or aging, depending upon the point of view!) may be discerned in an increasing number of analytical studies. However, theory and analysis, like ideology and methodology, are separable only in the abstract (see Polzin: 34/15/).

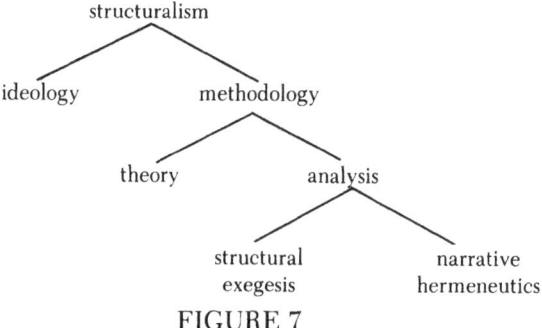

FIGURE 7

Just as structuralism as methodology bifurcates into theory and analysis, so structuralism as analysis subdivides into structural exegesis and narrative hermeneutics. In relationship to ideology, both theory and analysis are forms of methodology. In relationship to theory, both structural exegesis and narrative hermeneutics are forms of analysis. As theory is, in a sense, applied ideology, so structural exegesis is theory applied to an "object" (a text) and narrative hermeneutics is structural exegesis applied to a "subject" (a reader)/16/. Edgar McKnight's *Meaning in Texts: The Historical Shaping of a Narrative Hermeneutics*, from which I have borrowed the term "narrative hermeneutics," well represents this goal of structuralism. Structural exegesis as a goal of structuralism has been the aim of the present study of 1 Thessalonians.

These four—ideology, theory, structural exegesis, narrative hermeneutics—may be considered terminal goals of structuralism/17/; a structuralist may choose any one of them as her or his ultimate goal, though she or he may reach it via another goal (or goals) as penultimate/18/. Thus, in the *Mythologiques*, Lévi-Strauss moves from an analysis of individual myths (structural exegesis) to a theory of myth to an ideological understanding of what makes humanity human. In *Structural Exegesis: From Theory to Practice*, Daniel Patte and Aline Patte move from a semiotic theory to a structural exegesis of Mark 15 and 16, toward a narrative hermeneutic. In the present study, I have presupposed Lévi-Strauss's theory of myth as the basis for a structural exegesis of 1 Thessalonians.

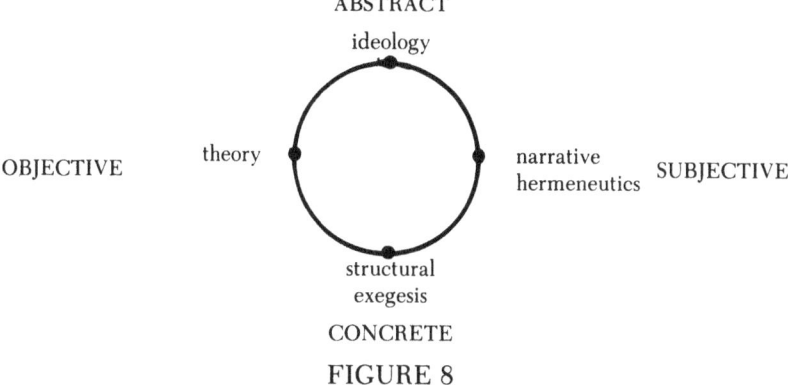

FIGURE 8

In actuality, both Lévi-Strauss and Patte and Patte move back and forth between goals, or forms of structuralism, in the process of discovering meaning. However, their respective directions and ultimate goals are clear: Lévi-Strauss moves toward ideology, Patte and Patte toward hermeneutics. Yet ideology and narrative hermeneutics are not as unrelated as they might appear from figure 7 above. The desire to philosophize on the basis of ethnography is not unlike the desire to theologize on the basis of narratology. Ideology, in its philosophical aspects, and narrative hermeneutics, in its theologica aspects, share a concern for the breadth of humanity and the depth of human beings/19/. It is possible that the continuum which might be represented as a line:

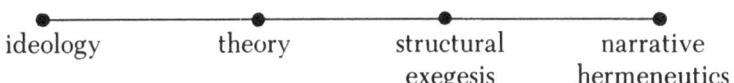

should be represented as a circle (see figure 8). For while movement from structural exegesis to theory to ideology (Lévi-Strauss) is movement from the concrete to the increasingly abstract—through the pole of the objective, movement from theory to structural exegesis to narrative hermeneutics (Patte and Patte) is movement from the objective to the increasingly subjective—through the pole of the concrete. Although I began my study with a theory developed by Lévi-Strauss, I have moved in a direction more similar to that of Patte and Patte: from a *theory* of myth to a *structural exegesis* of 1 Thessalonians.

B. FOCI

As structuralism as a whole may be approached, though not defined, by interrelating its diverse goals, so the various manifestations of structural criticism may be characterized by noting their distinctive foci. Based on the model of communication as the interrelation of Sender, Sign, and Receiver, a work of literature (in the broadest sense of the term) may be considered as the interrelation of Author, Text, and Reader. If the communication model is expanded to include Referent/20/—someone (Sender) says something (Sign) to someone (Receiver) about something (Referent)—the model of a literary work may be expanded to include World/21/. (See figure 9.) However, just as the four structuralist goals were seen to be non-exclusive, the four structuralist foci are interrelated in structural criticism. While one of the four elements (Author, Text, Reader, World) or one relation (e.g., Text-World or Text-Reader) may be of focal importance for a particular structuralist endeavor, all the elements and relations are of subsidiary importance, for the literary work as a whole. Thus the diagram (figure 9) might be conceived as a spider's web; touching one point or one strand causes the whole to vibrate. In addition, each of the four major foci may be further subdivided, for example:

>   Author—historical writer/incarnate narrator
>   Reader—particular reader/implied reader
>   World—historical world/literary world/22/.

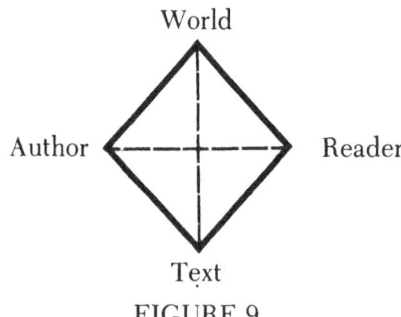

FIGURE 9

The Text is the shared focus of various methods of structural exegesis; to distinguish among these approaches we must first distinguish foci *within* the Text as focus. The text as sign has two levels: surface (narrative or epistolary) and depth (mythic)/23/. In traditional literary terms, the narrative level has to do with the characters and the plot; it is what makes the story recognizable as a story. In traditional form-critical terms, the epistolary level concerns the formulae of and divisions between salutation, body, and closing; it is what makes the letter recognizable as a letter. The mythic level has to do with the broader cultural, philosophical, religious significance of the text. The text as language (Saussure's *langue*), or a system of signs, has two dimensions: syntagmatic and paradigmatic. In the synchronic dimension of a text, elements are ordered chronologically; in the paradigmatic dimension of a text, elements are ordered abstractly, theoretically. Interrelating these two levels and two dimensions yields four textual foci:

(1) the syntagmatic dimension of the surface level
(2) the paradigmatic dimension of the surface level
(3) the syntagmatic dimension of the depth level
(4) the paradigmatic dimension of the depth level

which may be represented as in figure 10/24/.

TEXTUAL FOCI		dimensions	
		syntagmatic	paradigmatic
levels	surface	1	2
	depth	3	4

FIGURE 10

To concretize this abstract description of textual foci we may attempt to identify the foci of Propp, Lévi-Strauss, and Greimas as they analyze narrative texts and of Doty, White, and Funk as they analyze epistolary texts. Propp's focus on the order of invariant "functions" (types of actions) within the plot is a focus on the syntagmatic dimension of the narrative (surface) level (1). Lévi-Strauss's insistence that to "understand" a mythic text we must examine its bundles of relations arranged not chronologically but abstractly, in terms of opposition and mediation, is a focus on the paradigmatic dimension of the mythic (depth) level (4). The complex and ongoing work of Greimas is less easy to plot; however, two of Greimas's chief interests have been the actantial model and the constitutional model (or elementary structure of signification), and these represent, respectively, a focus on the paradigmatic dimension of the narrative (surface) level (2) and a focus on the paradigmatic dimension of the mythic (depth) level (4). Both Doty and White are concerned with establishing a theoretical model of the Pauline letter from beginning to end; thus their focus is the syntagmatic dimension of the epistolary (surface) level (1). While Funk shares this concern with Doty and White, he concentrates on one aspect of the letter form, the so-called "travelogue," in terms of its "logical," theoretical order and significance as "the apostolic *parousia.*" Thus Funk's major focus is the paradigmatic dimension of the epistolary (surface) level (2).

The present study of 1 Thessalonians, while focusing on the mythic (depth) level in both its syntagmatic (3) and paradigmatic (4) dimensions, has aimed for an awareness of the interrelation of all four aspects. To observe that at the beginning (1:1), middle (3:11–13), and end (5:12–22,

23–24; 5:25–28) of 1 Thessalonians the epistolary level is dominant is to examine the syntagmatic dimension of the epistolary (surface) level (1). To call attention to the functional parallelism between 1:1 and 5:25–18 as marks of the relationship between Paul and the Thessalonians and between 3:11–13 and 5:12–22, 23–24 as marks of the interrelation of thanksgiving and exhortation is to note the paradigmatic dimension of the epistolary (surface) level (2), although in 1 Thessalonians, as in all texts, the syntagmatic and paradigmatic dimensions are intricately interwoven. Isolation of the repeating pattern—[1] asserted (Objective) Knowledge, [2] enacted Demonstration/Explanation, [3] asserted Explanation/Demonstration, and [4] (subjective) knowing Action—develops from a study of the syntagmatic dimension of the mythic (depth) level (3). Analysis of the interrelation of the above four elements [1 : 2 :: 3 : 4] rests on an examination of the paradigmatic dimension of the mythic (depth) level (4).

Foci are the *what* of structural criticism, the aspects and relations for careful investigation. Goals are the *why* of structuralism, the purposes and reasons for careful investigation. Together goals and foci suggest a framework within which structural criticism operates, a typology of structural approaches to texts. We noted above that Propp, Lévi-Strauss, and Greimas all share a common goal in their structural research—theory, although they theorize on various topics (Russian fairy tales, kinship and myth, narrativity). Thus my differentiation of the goals of structuralism functions to link these three key figures, although it also differentiates Lévi-Strauss on the basis of his ideological aims. However, we have just noted that the three scholars, in their structural analyses of texts, focus on different aspects of the structure of texts. Thus my differentiation of textual foci functions to differentiate these key figures, although it does not illustrate their commonality as theorists. Likewise, Doty, White, and Funk share "theory" as a goal and "the syntagmatic dimension of the epistolary level" as a focus, but Funk is distinguished by a further concern for the paradigmatic dimension of the epistolary level. Thus, by establishing a typology of goals and foci, it is possible to register both commonalities and distinctions among major structuralist critics of narrative on the one hand and among critics of letters on the other. (See figure 11/25/ and figure 12.)

IV. CONCLUSION

As parallel figures, figures 11 and 12 illustrate the basic similarities between narrative texts and epistolary texts as *texts*: (1) they are two-leveled (surface/depth), and (2) each level is organized in two ways (syntagmatically/paradigmatically). The remaining questions are substantial

STUDY OF NARRATIVE TEXTS		foci			
		narrative/ syntagmatic	narrative/ paradigmatic	mythic/ syntagmatic	mythic/ paradigmatic
goals	ideology				Lévi-Strauss
	theory	Propp	Greimas		Lévi-Strauss Greimas
	structural exegesis				
	narrative hermeneutics				

FIGURE 11

STUDY OF EPISTOLARY TEXTS		foci			
		epistolary/ syntagmatic	epistolary/ paradigmatic	mythic/ syntagmatic	mythic/ paradigmatic
goals	ideology				
	theory	Doty White Funk	Funk		
	structural exegesis			(Malbon)	(Malbon)
	hermeneutics				

FIGURE 12

ones: Given these similarities, what differences exist between narrative texts and epistolary texts? How are narrative texts and epistolary texts to be related? It would appear that brief narratives are easily incorporated into letters (e.g., 1 Thessalonians 3:1–5) and that brief letters are easily incorporated into narratives (e.g., Acts 23:26–30). However, may a letter as a whole be conceived as a "narrative" (a story) of the relationship of a sender and a receiver? May a narrative as a whole be conceived as a "letter" (a message) from a writer/teller to a reader/hearer? How is the relationship between surface and depth to be understood? Is the "surface" level of a text (either a narrative or an epistolary level in the texts examined to this point) a "generic" level? Is the "depth" level of a text (a mythic level in the texts examined to this point) a "universal" level of communication?

The present study has focused on both the syntagmatic and the paradigmatic dimensions of the mythic level of Paul's letter to the Thessalonians and has had as its goal a structural exegesis of 1 Thessalonians. Structural exegesis, like any exegesis which seeks to avoid eisegesis, must finally be evaluated in terms of the text whose meaning it seeks to "draw out." 1 Thessalonians suggests that communication is an ongoing action, not a static state; the present structural exegesis of 1 Thessalonians is certainly an open-ended project, not a *fait accompli*.

NOTES

/1/ The distinction between "syntagmatic" and "paradigmatic," of course, grows out of the work of Saussure, although "paradigmatic" is actually Hjelmslev's term, Saussure's term "associative" being more problematic and less widely employed.

/2/ The text employed for this study is that of *The Greek New Testament*, ed. Kurt Aland et al., 3rd ed. (N.p.: United Bible Societies, 1975). Unless otherwise noted, quotations presented in English are from the Revised Standard Version of the New Testament, second edition, copyrighted 1971 by the Division of Christian Education of the National Council of the Churches of Christ in the United States of America.

/3/ With Best (73), I take the *hoti* in 1:5 to be epexegetical rather than causal and verse 5 to be explanatory of verse 4.

/4/ This is not to say that the occurrences of *parakaleō* (2:12; 3:2; 3:7) and *paraklēsis* (2:3) in the first half of the letter are unimportant. *Paraklēsis* at 2:3 seems especially important as a key term for Paul's overall ministry. That chapters 1–3 center on "thanksgiving" and chapters 4–5 center on "exhortation" is a common observation of 1 Thessalonians, and it is not made simply on the basis of the occurrence of the terms *eucharistia* and *paraklēsis*.

/5/ I do not propose to explicate Lévi-Strauss's formula in detail in this paper. For further discussion and applications the reader is referred to Patte, 1975:221–42; Polzin; Malbon, 1979:97–132. Both Polzin's book and my article take into consideration the adaptation of Lévi-Strauss's formula by Maranda and Maranda, who develop the image of mythic structure as helicoidal. Questions remain concerning the extent to which Lévi-Strauss's intent is modified by Maranda and Maranda's adaptation.

/6/ Cf. the references to *mnēoneuō* (1:3; 2:9), *ginōskō* (3:5), and *agnoeō* (4:13): 1:3, Paul remembers how the Thessalonians acted; 2:9, the Thessalonians remember how Paul acted; 3:5, Paul seeks to move from not knowing how the Thessalonians are faring to knowing how they are faring; 4:13, Paul seeks to move the Thessalonians from not knowing what will happen to those who have died to knowing what will happen to them.

/7/ Funk (1967:263-64), White (10-11), and Doty (11-12) each present a brief review of Heikki Koskenniemi, *Studien zur Idee und Phraseologie des briechischen Briefes bis 400 n. Chr.* (Helsinki: Suomalaien Tiedeakatemia, 1956). Koskenniemi argues that three basic motifs or functions of the Greek letter are (1) *philophronesis*, (2) *parousia*, and (3) *homilia*. As Doty explains, *philophronesis* refers to the purpose of the letter to express "the friendly relationship" between persons; *parousia* refers to the intention of the letter "to revive the existence of a friendship when the correspondents were physically separated"; *homilia* designates "the main function of the letter, the continuance of a dialogic conversation in writing."

/8/ As part of an analysis of paradigmatic structure one might also take a look at (1) the familial metaphors applied to the "actors" involved in these actions and (2) the temporal framework in which these actions are embedded. See Malbon, 1980:314-18.

/9/ I am using these terms interchangeably, although some writers do make a distinction between the two.

/10/ Lane expresses these two categories not as ideology and methodology but as "theories" and "methods"; but note Lane's use of the terms "philosophies and methods" (17) and "ideology" (18).

/11/ I do not mean by this to ignore the possible distinctions between ideology and philosophy, but rather to refer, in general and with neutrality, to what Robert Scholes identifies and Robert Polzin affirms as "structuralism as a movement of mind" (Scholes: 1; Polzin: iv, 1).

/12/ Lane is here describing what he terms a "theory" as opposed to a "method." See note 10 above.

/13/ Cf. Scholes's discussion of "structuralism as a movement of mind" and structuralism as a method (1-12). See also Culley: 169.

/14/ This distinction between theory and analysis is paralleled by Patte and Patte's distinction between "theory" and "practice" or "fundamental research" and "applied research" (10) and by Patte's distinction between the search for "universal structures" and the search for "structures which characterize each specific narrative" (1980:7).

/15/ Patte's discussion of "five types of structuralist research" (1980:7-9) may be understood as a development of the various relationships between theory and analysis: analysis in disregard of theory (Patte's type 1); theory in isolation from analysis (type 2); analysis for the sake of theory, whether inductive or deductive (types 3 and 4); and analysis in the light of theory (type 5).

/16/ Cf. Patte, 1976:3-6 on "exegesis" and "hermeneutic." See also Patte and Patte: vii, 94; and Patte, 1980:22.

/17/ My diagram of goals, although developed independently of Philip Pettit's "tree of options on which the structuralist analyst of narrative must decide his position" (54), may be fruitfully compared and contrasted with it. However, Pettit's tree of options serves as an evaluative tool (54-64): according to Pettit, theory fails—generative theory more drastically so than descriptive theory, and straight analysis is uncontrolled, thus only systematic analysis is workable; there is only one real option for structuralism.

/18/ Compare and contrast the five levels of the "problematic," or conceptual framework, of structuralism—or of any theoretical system—suggested by Miriam Glucksmann.

Listed according to "descending levels of abstraction rather than a hierarchy of determinacy" (10), they are: (1) epistemology, (2) philosophy, (3) theory, (4) methodology, (5) description. Glucksmann stresses that "each coherent thought system includes the five mentioned in some form" (10).

/19/ See Patte and Patte's diagram of "the path taken by Lévi-Strauss" and the path they follow to the "semantic universe" (15–16).

/20/ Suggestive to me at this point have been conversations with, and an unpublished paper by, Gary Phillips, now of the College of the Holy Cross, Worcester, Massachusetts. In "Ideology of the Sign" (Nashville, 1977), Phillips places an adaptation of Stephen Ullmann's model of the sign within Eugene Nida's schema of communication in order to account for both the linguistic reality and the extra-lingusitic reality of communication.

/21/ It is possible that the four points of figure 9 correspond to Patte's enumeration of three types of "constraints" upon a work of literature: (1) structures of the enunciation (Author), (2) cultural structures or cultural codes (World), and (3) deep structures (Text), and Patte's category of hermeneutics (Reader) (1976:22–23, 3–6). It would probably be more accurate to say that Patte's three types of constraints and his category of hermeneutics correspond to four relations as follows:

(1) structures of the enunciation/Author–Text relation
(2) cultural codes/World–Text relation
(3) deep structures/Text–Texts relation
(4) hermeneutics/Text–Reader relation

It would also appear that the two axes of figure 9 (broken lines) correspond to Patte's twofold categorization of the interests of structuralist research: signification systems (Text-World axis) and the communication process (Author-Reader axis). As the two axes of figure 9 intersect, so Patte's two categories are interrelated (1980).

/22/ Compare the model of the "coordinates of art criticism" (work, artist, audience, universe) presented by Abrams (especially 6), and the "maps" for literary critics (central point: work; cardinal points: author, reader, information, language) presented by Hernadi.

/23/ Greimas and others make a distinction between the "narrative" and the "discursive" dimensions of a text. Although, for purposes of comparing the work of Propp, Lévi-Strauss, and Greimas (see below), I have employed the term "mythic" rather than "discursive," the most significant difference between Greimas's distinction and my own is not merely terminological. For Greimas the narrative dimension is organized paradigmatically. Patte follows Greimas on this point. In *What Is Structural Exegesis?*, Patte discusses "the narrative and the mythical system" as "two semiological systems which have been sufficiently identified so that we can now begin to study them systematically at the levels of their structures of content" (34), although he does not assert that they are the only or the most basic semiological systems. In *Structural Exegesis: From Theory to Practice*, Patte and Patte elaborate systems on eight levels (1–38; see especially the figure on 15), the first four of which I would classify as sub-levels on the narrative level, the second four as sub-levels of the mythic level. In "One Text: Several Structures," Patte orders the various levels into two categories: syntagmatic systems (basically the first four levels) and paradigmatic systems (basically the second four levels). (Lévi-Strauss may be in line with this way of thinking as well, for he identifies the syntagmatic dimension with the "apparent" content and the paradigmatic dimension with the "latent" content.) Thus both Greimas and Patte collapse into a single distinction (variously labeled) aspects and relationships which I am suggesting may only be seen clearly in terms of two intersecting distinctions (narrative/mythic and syntagmatic/paradigmatic); see below. The terms "narrative"/"epistolary" and "mythic" are not at the same level of abstraction or generalization as "syntagmatic" and "paradigmatic"; they would not necessarily serve for all texts. "Surface" and "depth" serve as terms at the appropriate level of abstraction and generalization. However, in addition to their ambiguity, these metaphorical terms are laden with evaluative connotations. On the problems of the terms "surface" and "depth," see Polzin: 158-60. On the problems of studying "surface structure" and "deep structure," see Tannehill: 31-36. On the possibilities of the terms "surface" (perceptual order) and "depth" (imaginative order) in analyzing aesthetic experience, see Kaelin.

/24/ A more complete figure—in which "elements of the substance" (at both the surface and the depth levels) are distinguished from "formal relations," i.e., syntagmatic and paradigmatic relations (at both the surface and the depth levels)—from which figure 10 might be said to be "abstracted," is presented in Malbon, 1980:334-35, n. 49. However, because structural exegesis focuses on relations rather than on elements, this "expansion" is not necessary for our present purpose of systematizing the foci of structural exegesis.

/25/ Although developed independently (yet out of some shared contexts), Daniel Patte's table of "the broad categories of structuralist research" (1980:12) and my figure 13 are comparable. Patte's "structural exegesis" and my "structural exegesis" are identical, and his "semiotic research" and my "theory" are equivalent. My chart includes two additional categories along this dimension: "ideology" and "narrative hermeneutics," equivalents of which are spoken of by Patte in other contexts. Patte's categorization of the objects of study, "signification systems"/"communication process," corresponds with the two axes of my model of a literary work, Text-World/Author-Reader, as suggested above. Patte's table does not illustrate, but his discussion explicates, the distinction between "two types of signification systems: the syntagmatic and paradigmatic systems"; the distinction between syntagmatic and paradigmatic dimensions is illustrated in my chart. Neither Patte's table nor his accompanying explanation considers the distinction between the narrative and mythic (surface and depth) levels of the text, which my chart does illustrate. Patte has elsewhere (1976:34) stated his view that the narrative and the mythic are but two of the "semiological systems" of a text, so, perhaps, narrative and mythic structures could be considered as examples of the "universal structures" of Patte's table. However, it is my impression (see note 23 above) that Patte collapses into one distinction relationships which I am suggesting may only be seen clearly in terms of two intersecting distinctions (narrative/mythic *and* syntagmatic/paradigmatic).

METHOD FOR A STRUCTURAL EXEGESIS OF DIDACTIC DISCOURSES. ANALYSIS OF 1 THESSALONIANS

Daniel Patte
Vanderbilt University

Precis

The goal of this essay is to establish a method of structural exegesis aimed at elucidating the "system of convictions" (fundamental and "narrative" semantic systems) of didactic texts such as Paul's letters. For this purpose, we first consider the characteristics of didactic discourses, showing in the process their differences as compared with narratives. On the basis of this theoretical proposal (a semiotic model), a methodology is proposed. The validity of this model and of this methodology is then tested through the analysis of 1 Thessalonians. This analysis is not a structural exegesis *per se*, but the necessary step toward the establishment of the characteristics of the "faith" (system of convictions) of the author of this letter.

I. INTRODUCTION

1 Thessalonians, together with the other New Testament letters, presents structural exegetes with a new challenge. Indeed, their methods, which have been devised for the study of *narrative* texts (parables, Old Testament narratives, Gospels), cannot be directly applied to argumentative discourses—in fact, didactic discourses—such as Paul's letters. The question is then: Can we adapt for the study of non-narrative texts the existing set of structural exegetical methods, or do we need radically different methods? Before answering this question let us keep in mind what are structural exegetical methods and how they were (and are) developed on the basis of semiotic and structural theories.

For the exegetes, the first task was, of course, to familiarize themselves with the research in semiotics and structuralism. Narrative theories (based upon studies of folktales and myths, and later of narrative literary texts) were quite clearly the most elaborated theories. Thus for the biblical exegetes the question was: "How can we use these theories toward an exegetical end?" For my part, I concluded that *one* of the possible applications of these theories—and especially of Greimas's semiotic theory—is the study of the "systems of convictions" (the "fundamental and narrative semantics" according to Greimas's terminology) manifested by narrative biblical texts. I chose this particular exegetical goal because, in my view, it would allow us to describe "what characterizes the *faith* expressed by a text" understood as one of the dimensions of meaning of this text. Obviously, this does not exclude other possible applications of semiotic and structural methodologies pursuing other exegetical goals related to other dimensions of meaning of these texts (as is shown by the studies presented in *Semeia* 18, *Genesis 2 and 3: Kaleidoscopic Structural Readings* and by the other essays in the present issue). More specifically, it does not exclude the study of discoursive dimensions of meaning (proposed above by G. Phillips and J. D. Crossan) which have as their ultimate exegetical goal the description of what I would call the hermeneutical principles manifested by the text.

The development of an exegetical structural method aimed at the description of the characteristics of the faith manifested by a narrative text demanded to transform a theoretical model (Greimas's semiotic theory about narrative) into an analytical method. For this purpose it was necessary to formulate appropriate criteria, a task which has demanded our involvement in semiotic theoretical research whenever an aspect of the theory necessary for the establishment of exegetical criteria had not been completely developed (because the researchers strived to develop other points more important for the construction of an overall theory). Consequently, the establishment of such an exegetical structural method necessarily involved a theoretical presentation and its justification/illustration in the form of analyses of texts. Yet, of course, these analyses do not have, as their main goal, exegetical results but rather the establishment of a methodology. The *exegetical* use of such a methodology is not content to describe the semantic organization of the text. It aims at showing what *characterizes* this organization in a given text—that is, what is peculiar about it—an endeavor which necessarily involves a comparative study. The specificity of the system of convictions manifested by a narrative text can appear only by contrast with other systems of convictions.

We have to follow a similar procedure for the establishment of an exegetical structural method for the study of Paul's letters aimed at the study of the characteristics of the faith (system of convictions) manifested by these texts. To begin with we need to understand what is the precise nature of the texts which belong to the category *didactic* discourse. We will do so by considering the elements of a semiotic of didactic discourses proposed by Greimas and his collaborators. We shall, of course, underscore the characteristic features of didactic discourses which can serve as anchor points for an analytical methodology aimed at the study of the semantic organization of these discourses. In order to develop this methodology we shall take advantage of the methodological research already done concerning narratives. For this purpose we shall investigate the relations between narratives and didactic discourses in order to determine if there are any elements of the methods for the structural exegesis of narratives which can be adapted for the study of Paul's letters (this is also one of the goals of E. Malbon's essay, cf. above). This reflection will allow us to formulate a "theoretical model" of the semiotic characteristics of didactic discourses by comparing them with narratives. On this basis we shall then formulate a method involving a series of specific analytical steps. Then it will remain to verify the validity of this method and of the model it involves. This is what we shall do in the second part of this essay. Our analysis of 1 Thessalonians will therefore be a verification and an illustration of the model and of the method. Yet it should be emphasized that this analysis does not present the exegetical results aimed at by the method, i.e., the study of the "system of convictions" which characterizes Paul's faith according to this letter. This analysis merely shows how the fundamental and "narrative" semantics of the text is *organized* in this didactic text, i.e., *how* Paul's system of convictions is manifested in that text. Beyond this analysis, in a comparative study of one kind or another, one needs to study the relations among the semantic units thus established, in order to discern the characteristic patterns they form, and to reflect upon their implications for the understanding of the central issues raised by Paul's letters. These results can be found in Chapter IV of D. Patte, *Paul's Faith and the Power of the Gospel: A Structural Introduction to the Pauline Letters* (a book which does not present the formal analysis and the detailed methodology discussed in this article, but merely, exegetical results reached through a comparative study of all the Pauline letters, and a simplified, and thus less complete, methodology).

II. TOWARD A SEMIOTIC THEORY OF DIDACTIC DISCOURSES

A. WHAT IS A DIDACTIC DISCOURSE?

When one compares 1 Thessalonians with the definition of "didactic" in an unabridged dictionary, it is clear that this letter belongs to the category of didactic discourses—"a sub-class of discourses which are characterized by their *efficiency* and which can be evaluated in terms of it" (Greimas, 1979:3, my translation). Didactic discourses, as discourses conveying information and instruction, can be viewed as "causing to learn" or better, as *causing to know*. As conveying moral teaching, precepts, principles, rules, didactic discourses can be viewed as "causing to act in certain ways" or better as *causing to do*. As conveying pleasure and entertainment, but also views of the world, and insights (in didactic poems, didactic writings, didactic paintings), didactic discourses can be viewed as having still another type of function: *causing to believe*.

These preliminary observations based upon the dictionary definition could lead us into thinking that we should distinguish among three different types of didactic discourses in terms of the kinds of manipulation ("causing to") they involve. Yet we do not want to exclude the possibility that these three types of manipulation be found in the same didactic discourse. This is why we prefer to speak of the *functions*, "causing to know," "causing to do," and "causing to believe," of a didactic discourse. At any rate it appears that a semiotic theory about didactic discourse needs to involve defining these three types of manipulation and showing their interrelation. In fact, one can quickly see that there are only two functions. Indeed, the distinction between causing to do and causing to know is not semiotically pertinent. Causing to know can be viewed as a special case of causing to do (a causing to do in the cognitive domain, such as causing to learn). Learning is necessarily active, i.e., a doing. But then what is the relation between "causing to know" and "causing to believe"? Could it be the case that any causing to do and causing to know always presuppose a manipulation of the type causing to believe? Such are some of the questions we need to address on the basis of already established semiotic theories.

Without reviewing in detail Greimas's and his collaborator Paolo Fabbri's semiotic theory about didactic discourse (see Greimas, 1979, and Fabbri, 1979) let us take note of the elements of this theory which will be necessary for the establishment of an exegetical method and that I present here using a minimum of technical vocabulary (for a complete discussion of Greimas's and Fabbri's proposals, see Patte, 1980).

As Fabbri points out (cf. Fabbri, 1979:9–14) by taking the example of a pedagogical discourse, a didactic discourse is *twofold,* and thus includes *two distinguishable levels*. One can understand the nature of these two levels by taking the example of a scientific didactic discourse, e.g., that of a chemistry high school textbook. In a given chapter the author wants *to cause the students to learn* certain information regarding a chemical component. It is easy to reconstruct in general terms how this chapter was written. The author's research involves studying various articles in scientific journals and technical books, and reaching a conclusion about the nature of this chemical component. Let us assume that this conclusion is identical with that of a given article that we can call the "scientific discourse of reference." Yet as is clear the didactic discourse is not a mere repetition (even in a simplified form) of the argument of the article. In fact, the "discourse of reference" needs to be recast so that the argument will be convincing to the intended audience; the warrants used in the scientific essay would be meaningless to the students and thus new warrants using elements of what high school students (are supposed to) know need to be used. Furthermore, the discourse has also to *convince the readers to learn* this information about this chemical component; otherwise, the readers will not be actively involved in the reading process—and passive reading is reading in vain. For this purpose also, the didactic discourse needs to recast the "scientific discourse of reference" into a new discourse, this time in order to show the importance, the usefulness, the interest that a knowledge of the specific nature of this chemical component can have. Once again, this needs to be expressed in terms of what is important, useful, and interesting from the students' perspective.

This is true of any didactic discourse aimed at causing to know and at causing to do. For instance, imagine a discourse aimed at "causing to go fishing" somebody who never did it. A part of the discourse will have to explain to this would-be fisherman all the steps involved in "going fishing," from selecting the proper fishing gear to cleaning and preserving the fish one has caught. Here the discourse of reference would be the "Manual of the Good Fisherman." Another part of the discourse will have to convince the addressee that it might be fun to go fishing and that the instructions are indeed valid (for instance, by introducing in the discourse of reference stories concerning the instructor's previous fishing expeditions).

We can thus conclude that a didactic discourse involves two levels:

(a) A presentation of the main argument; in the preceding examples, the description of various features of the chemical component and a presentation of the argument allowing to reach a given conclusion regarding the nature of this chemical component; or a description of the various steps necessary to insure a successful fishing expedition. We shall call this level the *dialogic level* because it involves *the relation between an* (explicit or implicit) *"I"*—the teacher, the author, the instructor—*and an* (explicit or implicit) *"you"*—the students, the readers, the would-be fisherman—*in the present of the dialogue*. These are the instructions by the "I" concerning the concrete or cognitive steps the "you" should follow to reach a given result or conclusion.

(b) A presentation of warrants for the main argument aimed at showing its validity and its value (importance, usefulness, etc.). This is what we shall call the *warranting level*. These warrants refer to the past experience of either the "I" or of the "you," to future implications of reaching the goal proposed by the didactic discourse (the future use which one could make of this knowledge; eating fish after the fishing expedition), and/or to values or truth which have a general application (beyond the main performance of the action, learning or fishing, proposed; e.g., the fascination of scientific discovery, the fun and envigorating character of outdoor activities).

Greimas's theoretical proposal (cf. Greimas, 1979:1–8) helps us to understand more clearly the role and the interaction of these two levels. A didactic discourse of the type of "causing to do" (or "causing to know") aims at *establishing a "competent subject of doing (or knowing)"*: a student learning chemistry, a fisherman. As Greimas has shown, three modalities are necessary to insure the competence of a subject:

(1) *knowing*: he/she has to have the necessary knowledge;

(2) *being able to*: he/she has to have the ability to perform the action;

(3) *willing/wanting/having to*: he/she has to have the will to perform this action (whether this will is "free," a wanting, or a constraint, an obligation, a having to do).

The *dialogic level* of the discourse aims at establishing the addressees as knowing (and able) subjects. It provides the necessary knowledge in order to undertake the given activity, but also often suggests secondary activities aimed at obtaining skills or tools thanks to which the addressees will have the ability to perform the proposed task. For instance, the students might be invited to review a passage of a preceding chapter, the would-be fisherman might be instructed on how to practice casting.

The *warranting level* of the discourse aims at establishing the addressees as willing subjects. This is the "convincing" or "manipulating" dimension of the discourse. In fact, the warranting level also has two functions. On the one hand, it needs to establish subjects who will perceive the proposed action as something *desirable* (good, euphoric) and that they will be willing to do. On the other hand, it needs to establish subjects who will perceive the instructions as valid, and thus as trustworthy. For this latter purpose, the discourse needs to establish the reality/validity of the relation between "I" and "you" (instructor and instructed), as well as the reality/validity of the various steps proposed. In other words, the relation "I"/"you" and the instructions have to be made "plausible" by being shown to belong to a "real (plausible) world." In other words, the main argument of the dialogic level has to be inscribed in a "semantic universe" whose validity the addressees need to recognize. (A "semantic universe" is a specific perception of the "reality" of the world and of human experience which also specify what are the elements of this reality which are good and euphoric and thus desirable.) Insofar as the addressees accept this semantic universe they recognize for themselves the identity of willing subjects of the proposed program.

It is clear that, as long as the addressees are not established as willing subjects, the instructions (of the dialogic level) are useless. Now, note that accepting the validity of a semantic universe is nothing else than believing it. A semantic universe is indeed, as suggested above, a system of convictions. Without discussing here how the process of believing can be described semiotically (cf. D. Patte, 1982b), we can recognize that believing is a part of any action, and thus that any didactic discourse involves, to a greater or smaller extent, a "causing to believe" aimed at establishing a willing subject.

On the basis of these reflections one can envision a distinction between several types of didactic discourses:

(1) Didactic discourses which presuppose that the addressees have already the "right" semantic universe (i.e., the addresser's semantic universe). In such a case the warranting level can be very limited in scope. It is enough to show that the activity proposed (the dialogic level) is indeed inscribed in this semantic universe. In this case "causing to know" and "causing to do" are the dominant functions.

(2) Didactic discourses which presuppose that the addressees might not perceive the relationship between the proposed action and their own semantic universe (which is too narrow in scope, or weak, but not contradictory to that of the addressees). In such a case, a much more extensive warranting level is needed in order to show the relationship of each element of the dialogic level to the addressees' semantic universe. In extreme cases the warranting level can then constitute the quasi-totality of the didactic discourse. In other words, "causing to believe" becomes the dominant function, but "causing to do" remains the ultimate objective of the discourse.

(3) Finally, there are didactic discourses whose only objective is "causing to believe." They aim at communicating a different semantic universe to the addressees and thus at challenging an old semantic universe (and do not involve an explicit "causing to do" or "causing to know," since this would be useless before the new semantic universe is accepted). As we noted above, these are aesthetic didactic discourses (didactic poems, didactic writings, didactic paintings). Among these we find myths and also narratives of various types.

This last remark suggests that the latter type of discourse can be assimilated to either poetic discourse or to narratives. In the present essay, it is thus better to limit our investigation of didactic discourses to the first two types, leaving aside those of the type "causing to believe" (which would involve considering the didactic function of narratives). After all, Paul's letters always include exhortations and thus are discourses aiming at causing to do (and to know) and not merely at causing to believe. Yet these observations also bring us back into known territory by establishing a link between didactic discourse and narrative. The function "causing to believe," which is present to a greater or lesser degree in any didactic discourse, is the very function performed by narratives.

B. DIDACTIC DISCOURSE AND NARRATIVE

In the process of a research aimed at developing an exegetical structural method for the study of narrative, I have been led to make a distinction between two types of narratives: "profane" narratives which are iconoclastic in nature in that they aim at conveying a new vision of reality (a new system of convictions) and thus at challenging old visions; and "sacred" narratives which are aimed at strengthening and reaffirming an old vision ("strengthening the faith" of the addressees) (cf. D. and A. Patte, 1978:chapter IV). While the terminology could have been better chosen, this distinction is helpful for our understanding of didactic discourses because it is based upon the interrelations between the various narrative levels.

This is a first point of contact between narratives and didactic discourses. In a narrative we find a *main narrative level* and one (or several) *interpretative narrative levels*, i.e., narrative developments based upon an interpretation (by characters in the story) of the "value" of elements of the main narrative (for instance, in Mark, the people amazed by what Jesus did because they "see" in these events the intervention of God; then these people act according to this view). When we consider these narrative levels in terms of the above discussion of the levels in didactic discourses, it appears that *the main narrative level functions as a warranting level for the interpretative narrative level (which, in turn, corresponds to the dialogic level of a didactic discourse)*.

The above observation touches at what is, in my view, the essential difference between narrative and didactic discourses. I will express it using the "didactic discourse terminology." *In narratives,* the unfolding of the discourse (story) is commanded by the "warranting level" (the main narrative level to which the story comes back again and again). Conversely, the "dialogic level" of a narrative (the interpretative narrative level) is made out of textual elements which, while contributing to the development of the story, are "asides" diverging from the main story (without them the narrative would be semantically impoverished but would still make sense: it would remain a complete narrative development). In other words, in narratives the warranting level (the main narrative level) plays a predominant role and organizes the entire discourse. One can thus understand why narratives "cause to believe," since the function of a warranting level is to establish a semantic universe (a system of convictions).

By contrast, *in didactic discourses* (as defined above), we find the opposite interrelation of dialogic and warrantic levels. The dialogic level (interpretative level) commands the unfolding of the discourse: it aims at causing to do and thus at establishing what should be done and how to do it. The warranting level of a didactic discourse is made out of textual elements which, while contributing to the development of the discourse, "interrupt" the unfolding of the main argument (the dialogic argument). While the discourse might not be convincing without the warrants, it would still be a coherent and a complete argument (describing what to do and how to do it).

Once this essential difference between narratives and didactic discourses is recognized, it is easy to see that most of the methodology developed for the study of narratives also applies to the study of didactic discourses. This is apparent when one keeps in mind that the same syntactic and semantic structures can be invested by either abstract (cognitive) or concrete (somatic) contents. For instance, a "narrative" program, which involves the transmission of an object to a receiver by a subject, has the same structure in a narrative where these three actantial positions (or actants) are invested by personages and concrete objects and in a discourse where these might be invested by cognitive elements (ideas, etc.). In fact, this phenomenon is already found in narratives! The same is true of all the other structures. It is thus a matter of *adapting* the methodology developed for the study of narrative (presented in D. and A. Patte, *Structural Exegesis*, chapters II and III). We shall now present this methodology commenting on the differences with the methodology for the study of narrative as we progress.

C. A METHODOLOGY FOR THE STUDY OF DIDACTIC DISCOURSES

The methodology allowing to elucidate the organization of the fundamental semantic system of a didactic discourse—an analysis which is the necessary preliminary step for an exegetical study aimed at showing what characterizes the faith (system of convictions) manifested by this text—can be viewed as including the following steps. We describe them keeping the example of 1 Thessalonians in mind.

(1) *First step: Identification of the textual levels.*

The identification of the textual levels is easier in didactic discourse, as compared with narrative, because of the peculiar nature of the dialogical interpretative level. Indeed, one can begin by identifying the "dialogic space": the "I" and the "you" and how the "I" and "you" are defined by their relations with other "actors" in the present of the dialogue. (This is, in fact, a study of a part of the actorialization and temporalization as discussed by G. Phillips.) This "present" is a time span which includes both the present of the "I"—the time of writing—and the present of the "you"—the time when exhortations will be carried out. *All the textual elements which deal with the "I," the "you" and the actors associated with them in the present of the dialogue belong to the dialogic level.* The other textual elements, referring to other actors and/or to another time span, and/or to timeless truths, belong to the warranting level (or levels).

The warranting level might include (short) narratives. In such cases we can expect to find that the warranting level might have itself several levels (i.e., a main narrative level and one or several interpretative levels).

The identification of the warranting elements is often facilitated by textual markers introducing the warrants (such as "because"). Yet these markers are not sufficient in and of themselves because they might express other kinds of textual relations.

(2) *Second step. Identification of the system of pertinent transformations.*

As in the case of narratives, one can then proceed to the identification of the pertinent transformations. This is necessary because of the interrelations between syntactic organization and semantic organization: the organization of pertinent transformations (a syntactic system) provides a solid ground for the study of the semantic organization.

(a) A transformation is the relation between the object and the receiver (O ⟶ R) which is expressed by any verb of the category of doing (by contrast with the verbs of the category of being/having which express "states" rather than transformations). Note that reflexive verbs as well as verbs of feeling and cognitive verbs involve transformations. A specific character of didactic discourses is that often the transformations expressed are not completed: for instance, when they are expressed in an imperative form they remain potential, yet they have to be taken into account. Furthermore, transformations might be expressed in a nominal (rather than a verbal) form: such is the case of the nouns expressing "thematic roles" (such as "fisherman" in our example). This is one of the difficulties of interpretation: one has to judge whether or not such nouns emphasize the actor or the transformation. In the latter case they need to be included among the transformations manifested by the text.

(b) On each level the transformations belong either to the principal (usually positive) axis or to the polemical (usually negative) axis. One needs therefore to identify the axis to which each transformation belongs.

(c) On each level the text opposes certain transformations in pairs involving a transformation belonging to the principal axis, and another belonging to the polemical axis. These pairs of opposed transformations need to be identified because they are the syntactical manifestations of semantic oppositions. This is why we call them pertinent transformations: they are the text's way of calling attention to certain semantic relations.

Two transformations form a pair of opposed pertinent transformations:

(a) when these two transformations belong respectively to the principal and the polemical axis;

(b) When they have (1) *either* the same receivers (or comparable receivers, e.g., receivers belonging to the same category) and contradictory objects (i.e., objects which are opposed but belong to the same semantic field or isotopy); (2) *or* the same objects (or comparable objects) and contradictory receivers. Another possibility is that the two transformations involve the same receivers and the same objects but one is a positive transformation (doing something) and the other a negative transformation (not doing something). Yet note that in this latter case the non-performance of the transformation must be clearly manifested in the text (somebody not doing something); it cannot be merely a transformation which is not completed (when, e.g., it is not expressed whether or not an action has been carried out). This can be summarized in the formulas:

$$(O \longrightarrow R) \quad vs \quad (\overline{O} \longrightarrow R)$$
$$(O \longrightarrow R) \quad vs \quad (O \longrightarrow \overline{R})$$
$$(O \longrightarrow R) \quad vs \quad (O \not\longrightarrow R)$$

(d) Once the pairs of pertinent transformations of each textual level have been identified, the interrelation of these pairs needs to be elucidated (bracketing out of consideration all the other transformations and other syntactic features).

This is a most important step of the analysis since the syntactic organization of the system of pertinent transformations is reflecting the organization of the fundamental and "narrative" semantic system, i.e., the organization of the system of convictions manifested by the discourse. Indeed, even though the two systems are not *isomorphic* (they do not have exactly the same shape), they are *isotopic*. The semantic system can be viewed as the projection on another plane of the system of pertinent transformations. In this process, the structure of the system of pertinent transformations is submitted to a coherent deformation—to a warping—according to which the narrative *contrary* oppositions of the system of transformations become semantic *contradictory* oppositions of the semantic system manifested by the symbolic units (qualifications, etc.) attached to the pertinent transformations. Thus, in brief, as soon as we will have elucidated the organization of the system of pertinent transformations we will have for all practical purposes established the organization of the fundamental/narrative semantic system (and of the system of convictions).

In the case of narratives, the elucidation of the system of pertinent transformations is relatively straightforward. One begins by organizing the pairs of pertinent transformations of the main narrative level according to the logic governing the unfolding of the narrative development. Then one studies the various elements of the interpretative level(s) which, usually, are manifested in discrete interpretative textual units, establishing the mini-system of pertinent transformations of each unit and linking them with the transformations(s) of the main narrative level which correspond(s) to the point where these interpretative units diverge from the main narrative level (cf. D. and A. Patte, *Structural Exegesis*, chapter II and chapter III). In brief, the system of pertinent transformations of the main narrative level (which corresponds to one isotopy of the semantic system) is the "trunk" to which are attached various mini-systems of convictions of the interpretative level (which correspond to other isotopies of the semantic system). As such the semantic organization is closely related to the surface manifestation of a narrative whose development is governed by the main narrative level (the trunk) from which the interpretative textual units *branch out*.

In the case of didactic discourses, the semantic organization (and of the system of pertinent transformations) is less directly related to the surface manifestation of the discourse. In fact, we could say that it is "hidden," precisely because of the function of didactic discourses which aims at "manipulating" (convincing) the addressees to do something. It needs therefore to be "uncovered."

We have noted above, that the warranting level of a didactic discourse corresponds to the main narrative level of a narrative. This means that we need *to begin by establishing the system of pertinent transformations of the warranting level which form the "trunk" of the overall system of pertinent transformations.* Yet, as we have also noted, the warranting level does not usually form a coherent narrative development. It is rather made up of what can be viewed as fragments of a story which are located in the textual manifestations according to the needs of the dialogic level. In order to elucidate the organization of the system of pertinent transformations one needs therefore to organize the pairs of transformations according to the logic of the unfolding of this "reconstructed" story. In other words, one needs to organize the pairs of transformations according to their *syntactic* relations (especially, cause and effect relations, which are also expressed as temporal relations—since the cause and effect relations of the surface narrative syntax are often manifested by the temporalization of the discoursive syntax). (For the differences between these two kinds of syntax see D. Patte, "Greimas's Model of the Trajectory of Meaning in Discourse," 1982a:59–78.) As the analysis of 1 Thessalonians shows, this operation is in fact much easier to perform than it sounds and is, in no way, arbitrary. We will explain other criteria for this part of the analysis when presenting this example.

Once the system of pertinent transformations of the warranting level is established, one needs to consider the various units of the dialogic level in order to establish the mini-system of pertinent transformations which they manifest and attach them (as branching out of the system of pertinent transformations of the warranting level) to the transformations of the warranting level to which they are connected by the discourse. Often this connection is explicit: certain exhortations are directly related to a given warrant (a part of the warranting level). In such a case there is no difficulty. In other cases where this connection is not explicit, one needs to take into account thematic relations (as will be illustrated by the analysis of 1 Thessalonians).

(3) *Third Step: Semantic Analysis*

When the overall system of pertinent transformations is elucidated one can proceed exactly as for the analysis of narrative. From the organization of the system of pertinent transformations, one can derive the "symbolic system" which interrelates, in a series of interrelated semiotic squares, the symbolic units which are manifested in the discourse by the bundles of qualifications and of utterances of state associated with the pertinent transformations.

By studying the interrelations of these symbolic units one can then show what are the semantic features which set them in relations of contrariety, of contradiction and of implication the one with the others. But, once more, the significance of this semantic system (and of the semantic relations it involves) appears only through a comparative study.

III. STRUCTURAL ANALYSIS OF 1 THESSALONIANS

A. THE GOALS OF OUR ANALYSIS OF 1 THESSALONIANS

In the following analysis of 1 Thessalonians we do not aim at exegetical results. We want simply to verify the validity of the model and of the analytical method described above. In other words, we want simply to show that the various relations *which characterize*, in our view, *any didactic discourse*, can indeed be found in this letter. In the process many of the above theoretical points will appear more concretely. Thus our attention is *not* focused on what characterizes 1 Thessalonians (the goal of an exegetical study). Furthermore, since the model for didactic discourses and the corresponding methodology does not differ from those about narratives at the stage of the semantic analysis, we shall not present this last stage of the analysis in detail; one can follow on this point the example provided in D. and A. Patte, *Structural Exegesis from Theory to Practice*. Indeed, by the following detailed analysis we want to present an example of the structural analysis of a didactic discourse which can be used for the analysis of other didactic discourses. And thus we emphasize only the peculiar features that the methodology has as compared with the methodology for narrative analysis.

While this analysis of 1 Thessalonians following this method does not provide direct exegetical results, it must be used to reach exegetical results concerning the characteristics of the faith (system of convictions) of the author. The same method needs then to be used for the study of other letters so that a valid and fruitful comparison of these might be performed concerning this dimension of their meaning. The comparison with other Pauline letters allows us to show the characteristics of Paul's faith; this is what I have chosen to do in *Paul's Faith and the Power of the Gospel*. The comparison with letters whose Pauline authorship is dubious, might allow us to provide other arguments for or against their

Pauline authorship. The comparison with other didactic discourses will allow us to show the differences between these discourses in terms of the faith of their respective "authors."

B. THE TEXTUAL LEVELS OF 1 THESSALONIANS

(1) *1:1–3a. The Opening of the Letter* is clearly "dialogic." It manifests the dialogic relation between the author and the readers, that is, Paul as addressing the Thessalonians by means of this letter, and the Thessalonians as addressed by this letter. It might be good to emphasize here that the dialogic level does *not* include the elements of Paul's and the Thessalonians' stories outside of the dialogical relation manifested by the letter, that is the elements referring to events which are either past or future by comparison with the letter and its direct effect upon the readers. It is necessary to insist on this point here because the same characters are involved throughout the letter, so much so that the distinction between the levels is blurred. Yet here again we have to yield to V. Propp's warning that characters are *not* pertinent units of the formal semantic organization of a text.

(2) *1:3b–3:6. The Warranting Section of the Letter.* The following section of the text, 1:3b to 3:6 (except for some verses and phrases which will be discussed below) proposes various elements of past stories which warrant Paul's thanksgiving and exhortations. We can readily observe that this warranting section is framed by two statements about thanksgiving which echo each other:

1:2,3 "We give thanks to God always for you all, constantly mentioning you in our prayers, remembering before our God and Father your work of faith. . . ."

3:7–10 "For this reason, brethren, in all our distress and affliction we have been comforted about you through your faith; for now we live, if you stand fast in the Lord. For what thanksgiving can we render to God for you for all the joy which we feel for your sake before our God, praying earnestly. . . ."

The three major features of the first passage—thanksgiving to God, prayers related to the Thessalonians, and mention that the reason for the thanksgiving is the Thessalonians' faith—can be found in the latter passage. A reference to thanksgiving is also found in 2:13 (approximately the center of this section) as if to remind the readers that this recounting of various events is intended to explain the reasons for Paul's thanksgiving. Thus it is clear that one of the functions of the warranting section is to provide the basis for the thanksgiving which is then prolonged by the exhortations found in 3:11–5:28 which belong to the dialogic level (except for some verses and phrases which will be discussed below).

A closer examination of the warranting section soon reveals that it has certainly other functions as well. First we can note that the warranting section found in 1:3b–3:6 is not a single unit—such as a story unfolding coherently according to a narrative logic. It is rather a very fragmented text made out of a series of elementary narratives which are not organized according to the need of a narrative development, but according to the need of the dialogic discourse which is manifested in this section of the text in the form of phrases which break down the warranting material into discrete units. Let us identify these units of the warranting level, which, as could be expected, have a narrative character (and can be viewed as elementary narratives):

1:3b–c is the expression, in a nominal form, of the work of faith, the love and the steadfastness of the Thessalonians. It is introduced by a phrase centered upon the verb "remembering" (*mnēmoneuontes*, 1:3a) which belongs to the dialogic level.

1:4 is the expression, in a nominal form, of God's action vis-a-vis the Thessalonians: he loves them and elected them. (Thus this verse can be termed: the story of God and the Thessalonians.) It is introduced by the phrase of the dialogic level, "we know" (*eidotes*, 1:4a).

1:5–6 is the story of Paul's proclamation of the Gospel to the Thessalonians and their response. It includes the interpretative phrase "you know" (*kathōs oidate*, 1:5c) which emphasizes the brief description of Paul's attitude (1:5d).

1:7–8 is the story of the people who heard about the Thessalonians' acceptance of the Gospel. It can be viewed as a diverging (interpretative) elementary narrative based upon the preceding (1:5–6) and the following (1:9b–10a) passages. It forms therefore a secondary warranting level, which involves a reference to the fact that Paul does not need to say anything about this (which implies "we know").

1:9–10a is another expression of the story of the Thessalonians' response to the proclamation of the Gospel by Paul, introduced by "for they themselves report" (and thus "we know").

1:10b–d is a brief summary of the kerygma, i.e., the story involving Jesus, God and their relation to "us." As such the kerygma belongs to the primary warranting level.

2:1–14b is a story of the proclamation of the Gospel by Paul to the Thessalonians with emphasis on Paul's persecutions, motivations, and attitudes (2:1–12) followed by a new expression of the Thessalonians' acceptance of the Gospel and their persecution (2:13–14b). This story is complemented by a few converging narratives: 2:4 explaining Paul's general motivation when proclaiming the Gospel (he is "approved by God"); and 2:12e–g mentioning an element of the story of God's relation to the Thessalonians. We note also that the narrative elements are repeatedly introduced by interpretative phrases like, "as you know" (*kathōs oidate*, 2:1,2,5,11); "you remember" (*mnēmoneuete*, 2:9); "you are witnesses" (*hymeis martyres*, 2:10); and, "we also thank God constantly for this" (2:13a). All of these phrases are nothing else than elements of the dialogic level which are interjected in the warranting level and manifest once more that the various elements of the primary warranting level are organized according to the needs of the dialogic level of the discourse and not according to the logic of the narrative development of the units of the warranting level. Thus despite the relative coherence of the narrative development, this section of the text is nevertheless quite fragmented because of the narrative redundance.

2:14c-16c is a story of how the Jews killed Jesus and the prophets, and persecuted the church and Paul.

2:16d-e may be viewed as a brief diverging narrative story interpreting the value of 2:14c-16c. It belongs therefore to the secondary warranting level.

2:17-3:6 is the story of Paul's attempt to go and visit the Thessalonians, of the sending of Timothy and his return to Paul with news about the Thessalonians. This elementary narrative is the narrative prolongation of the story which Paul shared with the Thessalonians. 2:19-20, which expresses the motivations of Paul's attitude in the form of a value judgment concerning Paul's relation to the Thessalonians, shows that this is an interpretative prolongation. That is, 2:17-3:6 must be viewed as belonging to the secondary warranting level, except for a few verses and phrases.

This warranting unit manifests a development which is less fragmented than the one found in the preceding passages. It is nevertheless interrupted by 3:3c-4, a narrative describing what Paul taught the Thessalonians about persecutions which is framed by two phrases of the dialogic level, "you yourselves know . . . as you know" (3:3b and 3:4c). Thus 3:3e-4b belongs to the primary warranting level. Furthermore, 3:5c,d, which expresses what Paul would like to know about the situation of the Thessalonians (their faith or their being tempted by the Tempter) so as to prolong dialogically their story more adequately (either in thanksgiving or in the conclusion that he had worked in vain). Thus 3:5c,d manifests hypothetical elements of the primary warranting level.

(3) *3:7-5:28. The dialogic section of the letter.* The second part of the letter (even though it involves a few warranting units which will be discussed below) is primarily dialogic: it expresses the exhortations of "we" to "you." But here again we find a fragmented development, i.e., a series of converging textual units. The interjections of references to the warranting level in the dialogic discourse seems to have the same fragmenting effect as the interjections of dialogic elements in the warranting level described above. Let us consider each textual unit in turn:

3:7-11 is an interpretative prolongation of the warranting level, in which Paul expresses his thankfulness and his wish to visit the Thessalonians. Despite the similarity with 2:17:20 (which as past story belongs to the warranting level), this unit belongs to the dialogic level, since it manifests the dialogical relationship of the author and the readers (in the "present" of the letter). This unit is clearly the interpretative prolongation of the concluding part of the warranting level (Timothy's visit and report).

3:12–13 is correlated to the preceding textual unit. 3:7–11 expressed the interpretative prolongation of the warranting level insofar as it concerns what Paul does and wishes to do. 3:12–13 expresses now a similar prolongation focused this time on what the Thessalonians should do following Paul's example (loving as he does) and consequently on what should be their relationship to God and the Lord Jesus.

4:1–8. This exhortation to a life free from immorality is merely juxtaposed with the preceding unit: there is a thematic link (3:13 already includes a call to holiness) but there is a double break in the discoursive development from one to the other (there is no progression comparable to a progression in the narrative hierarchy nor an unfolding of discoursive development). In fact, this unit is introduced by and includes repeated references to a specific part of the warranting level expressed by the phrase, "as you learned from us" (*kathōs parelabete par' hēmon*, 4:1d), by v 2, "for you know what instructions we gave you through the Lord Jesus" (the phrase *oidate gar* signals here a reference to the warranting level), and by vv 6c–8: "because the Lord is our avenger in all these things, as we solemnly forewarned you. For God has not called us for uncleanness, but in holiness. Therefore whoever disregards this, disregards not man but God, who gives his Holy Spirit to you." The dialogic part of this passage is based upon an interpretation of the previous teaching of Paul to the Thessalonians briefly mentioned in 2:11–12. Thus in this textual unit we find two features: new elements of the warranting level (vv 1d, 2 and 6c–8) and a dialogic discourse which prolongs interpretatively this part of the warranting level.

4:9–12. This exhortation to the proper loving attitude is, as the preceding passage, without direct link with the other units of the dialogic level and includes references to the part of the warranting level it interprets: "for you yourselves have been taught by God to love one another; and indeed you do love all the brethren throughout Macedonia" (4:9b–10a). This warranting element is related to 2:13f,g ("the word of God which is at work in you believers") and 1:3b (the Thessalonians' "labor of love").

4:13–18. Once more this unit is simply juxtaposed to the preceding passages. It involves teachings concerning the brethren who died, concluded by an exhortation to "comfort one another" (4:18). It is the interpretative prolongation of a specific part of the Kerygma, Jesus' death and resurrection, cited in 4:14b,c, which belongs to the warranting level as we suggested earlier when dealing with 1:10b–d. With the exception of 14b,c, these verses belong to the dialogic level.

5:1-11. This pericope prolongs the preceding passage and, therefore, belongs to the same textual units although it is now based upon the interpretation of another part of the warranting level, the Thessalonians' knowledge about the Day of the Lord, which is cited in 5:2b-5b following the now familiar introductory phrase "for you yourselves know" (*autoi gar . . . oidate*, 5:2a) reinforced by the qualifier "very well" (*akribōs*). The text signals clearly where the interpretative didactic discourse is reintroduced by the phrase "so then" (*ara oun*, 5:6a).

5:12-28. The concluding section of the letter is made up of a series of juxtaposed and often very brief dialogic textual units without explicit reference to the elements of the primary narrative which are prolonged interpretatively in this fashion. We shall see that they are indeed related to the warranting level, but none of its elements are cited here. All the elements of these verses belong to the dialogic interpretative level. The following table shows in summary form to which textual levels the various passages belong. (See Table I).

C. THE SYSTEMS OF PERTINENT TRANSFORMATIONS OF THE WARRANTING LEVEL

The preceding study of the textual levels has been performed following a single set of criteria related to the breaks in the formal hierarchical pattern which characterizes the interrelation of the (narrative) programs and the breaks in the logical development. Although I have not discussed these programs for the sake of space, the preceding results have been obtained after an identification of all the (narrative) programs manifested by the text, so that their specific relations might be carefully studied. Yet, such a study still needs to be verified by considering the oppositions of transformations—a transformation being the part of a program symbolized by the relation ($0 \longrightarrow R$). The two terms of such oppositions necessarily belong to the same textual level. When two transformations are clearly in opposition (that is, having the same Object and contradictory Receiver or the same Receiver and contradictory Object, or again, the same Object and Receiver and opposed performances), and belong to two textual units which have been identified as belonging to different levels, the preliminary identification of the levels must be reexamined. The above comments have taken into account this second set of criteria. For the sake of verification, we have compared all the principal programs with all the polemical programs, without taking into account the levels, so as to verify our identification of these levels.

We do not need to describe this process here. In our presentation, we shall merely show the set of oppositions of pertinent transformations we have identified for each level at the conclusion of our analysis which involved successively: (a) the formal representation of each program; (b) the assignment of each program to one of the two (narrative) axes (i.e.,

TABLE I

WARRANTING LEVEL		DIALOGIC LEVEL
Primary Warranting Level	Secondary Warranting Level	
		−1:1−2 opening of letter Thanksgiving
−1:3b−c Thess' work of faith, love & steadfastness		−1:3a "remembering"
−1:4 God's action vis-a-vis Thess		−1:4a "we know"
−1:5−6 Paul's proclamation of Gospel to Thess		−1:5c "as you know"
	−1:7−8 people who heard about Thess' faith	
		−1:9a "For they themselves report" (= we know)
−1:9−10a Thess' response to Paul's proclamation		
−1:10b−d Jesus, God and their relation to "us"		
−2:1−14b Paul's proclamation of Gospel to Thess		−2:2, 5, 11 "as you know"
		−2:9 "you remember"
		−2:10 "you are witnesses"
		−2:13a "we also thank God constantly for this"
−2:14c−16c Jews killing Jesus, prophets, persecuting church & Paul		
	−2:16d−e God's wrath upon the Jews	
	−2:17−3:6 Paul's attempt to go and visit Thess; sending of Timothy & his report	
−3:3c−4 Paul's teaching about persecutions to Thess		−3:3b, 4c: "you yourselves know . . . as you know"
−3:5d hypothetical situation of Thess as tempted by the Tempter		
		−3:7−11 Paul's Thanksgiving and wish to visit Thess
		−3:12−13 what should be Thess' attitude f. Paul's example; their relation to Jesus
−4:1d, 2, 6c−8 Paul's earlier instructions about immorality and God's will		−4:(1−8) exhortation to a life free from immorality
−4:9b−10a God's instruction to love one another & Thess' response		−4:9−12 exhortation to the proper loving attitude
−4:14, b, c, Jesus' death & resurrection		−4:13−18 teaching and exhortation concerning the brethren who died
		−5:1−11 exhortation related to the Day of the Lord
−5:2b−5b Thess' previous knowledge about the Day of the Lord		
		−5:12−28 various exhortations, concluding blessing

either to the principal axis or to the polemical axis) which, in the present case, also correspond to the semantic axes; (c) the comparison of the principal transformations with the polemical transformations. In this discussion we shall follow the order of the text although, as we shall see, this order is not that of the system of pertinent transformations.

(1) *Identifying the Pertinent Transformations of the Warranting Level*

1:5b we-1 (Gospel ⟶ you)   vs.   1:5a we-1 (Gospel ⟶̸ you)

1:5 includes two transformations which are opposed. The first part of the verse (1:5a) expresses a hypothetical polemical transformation manifesting the non-communication of the Gospel: Paul and his associates (which I represent by "we-1," while "we-2" will be used to refer to Paul and the Thessalonians) has not communicated the Gospel to the Thessalonians (represented by "you") "only in word." This qualification is actually a manifestation of the Helper which Paul (and his associates) would have used for this communication (which did not take place). Since in our minimal representation of the program we only record the Subject, the Object, and the Receiver (in order to compare more easily the programs), the Helper "only in word" (*en logō monon*) is not represented. It is, of course, a very important symbolic manifestation of a semantic value which will be studied later on. In an elliptic way (the verb and its complement, *egenēthē eis hymas*, are not repeated), the second part of the verse expresses a principal program manifesting the communication of the Gospel when the Subject, we-1 has other Helpers ("in word" *and* "in power and in the Holy Spirit with full conviction," *kai en dynamei kai en pneumati agiō kai (en) plērophoria pollē*). These two transformations, which involve the same Object, the same Receiver and opposite performances (performance in the actual program, non-performance in the hypothetical program) form, therefore, a first pair of pertinent transformations. It is clear that its identification permits to localize in the text an important semantic opposition. We shall find other manifestations of this opposition (2:2e; 2:4d; 2:9d *vs.* 2:3a,b,c).

°1:8c you (news about Thess'   vs.   °1:8b (news about
   faith ⟶ people   Thess' faith ⟶ people in
   everywhere)   Macedonia and Achaia alone)

Similarly, in 1:8 two transformations (one actualized, the other hypothetical) concerning the communication of news about the Thessalonians' faith, are opposed. 1:8b expresses the hypothetical propagation of the "news about the Thessalonians' faith" (Object) to the "people in Macedonia and Achaia alone" (Receiver). By contrast, 1:8c expresses the same communication to "people everywhere" (Receiver).

1:9b (2:1b) you   vs. 2:2a,b Philippians (mistreatment
   (welcome ⟶ we-1)   and insults ⟶ we-1)

The welcome (O) that the Thessalonians (S) gave to Paul and his associates (R) (*hopoian eisodon eschomen pros hymas* 1:9b) is opposed to the mistreatments and insults (O) that Paul and his associates (R) received from the Philippians (2:2a,b).

1:9d you (self ⟶ God)   vs. 4:8c anyone (self ⟶̸ God)

Turning to God (1:9d) (and away from idols) is opposed to rejecting God (*athetei ton theon*, 4:8c). Both programs can indeed be viewed as manifesting reflexive actions: giving and not giving oneself (O) to God (R) or alternatively attributing and not attributing God (O) to oneself (R). All our analyses confirm that reflexive actions can be compared (and thus also opposed) to each other whatever might be their subjects. The specific manifestation of what we represent by "self" in the actantial position of either Object or Receiver is solely defined by the investments of the actantial position of the Subject and its qualifications (its Helpers) and thus must not be considered when studying the transformations—it will be accounted for in the study of the semantic system.

1:9e, "serving God," involves a program to which one could eventually oppose "displeasing God," 2:15d. But, as we shall see, the latter is more directly opposed to 2:12e "pleasing God," which, of course, is closely related to 1:9e.

1:10a (5:4a) you (expectation   vs. 5:4b you (surprise at Day
   of Lord's coming ⟶ you)   of the Lord ⟶ you)

This opposition is self-explanatory. Note simply that the Greek text emphasizes the negative program, as a hypothetical program which would take place if the Thessalonians were "in darkness," but they are not (the negation bears upon the qualification).

1:10b God (non-death ⟶ Jesus)   vs. 2:15b Jews (death ⟶ Jesus)

This pair is an example of the classic opposition of the hero's and the villain's action: the hero (in this instance, God) "undoing" what the villain (the Jews) has done. Note that we find another reference to the resurrection in 4:14b. Yet this second instance is concerned with the raising of Jesus (*aneste*) which must be represented as God (raised state ⟶ Jesus), despite the mention of Jesus' death which precedes, in order to respect the ambiguity of the phrase. By contrast in 1:10b, the phrase *egeiren ek (tōn) nekrōn* without ambiguity sets this program in direct opposition to the killing of Jesus.

2:2d (God/we-1) vs. 2:16a Jews (hindrance ⟶ we-1)
   (courage ⟶ we-1)

The attribution to Paul and his associates (we-1) of "courage" by God (or by Paul with God as Helper *eparrēsiametha en tō theō*, 2:2d) for the proclamation of the Gospel is opposed to hindering (the attribution of "hinderance") Paul's proclamations (2:16a). Note further that both in 2:2 and 2:16 the Receiver "we-1" becomes the Subject of the same program (proclamation of the Gospel to Gentiles) in the next step of the narrative hierarchy.

2:2e; we-1 (Gospel ⟶ you) vs. 2:3a,b,c we-1 (erroneous,
(also, 2:4d; 2:9d)   unclean, crafty
                                           message ⟶ you)

This opposition which is repeatedly manifested is, in fact, a duplication of the opposition we have recorded above, 1:5b *vs.* 1:5a.

2:4e we-1 (pleasing   vs. 2:4d we-1 (pleasing
   attitude ⟶ God)   attitude ⟶ man)

Let us note simply that, once more, one of the two opposed transformations is manifested elliptically: the verb *areskontes* is not repeated in 2:4e (compare 2:12e *vs.* 2:15d).

2:7b we-1 (gentleness ⟶ you) vs. 2:7a we-1 (authoritative
                                              attitude ⟶ you)

This opposition between two attitudes can be expressed in the form of transformations as proposed above despite the fact that it is manifested in the text by means of verbs belonging to the category of being/having. A methodological issue is at stake here. Is it appropriate to identify programs which are expressed in the text in other ways than through verbs of the category of "doing"? We believe this procedure to be adequate when dealing with non-narrative texts. Yet one needs to proceed with extreme caution: the interpretation of such phrases as transformations must be justified in terms of their role in narrative developments (narrative hierarchy). In the present case we keep it only because this opposition duplicates other oppositions (cf. Table IV, below).

2:8d we-1 (Gospel and our   vs. 2:8c we-1 (Gospel
   lives ⟶ you)   alone ⟶ you)

This opposition manifested elliptically is closely related to the preceding one: 2:8d appears to be another expression of the gentleness of Paul for the Thessalonians.

2:10c,d,e we-1 (holiness,   vs.   2:6b,c,d man, you,
righteousness, blameless-   others (praise ⟶ we-1)
ness ⟶ we-1)

2:10c,d,e manifests a threefold program despite the English translations which suggest a mere qualification (expressed by the copula "being"): the Greek *ginomai* does not denote a mere state (the result of a transformation) but a transformation (a becoming). The Objects "holiness, righteousness and blamelessness" (manifested by *hosiōs, dikaiōs, amemptōs*) on the one hand, and "praise" or "glory" (*doxa*) on the other are contradictory in that they concern opposed qualifications belonging to the same isotopic space (the isotopic space of the moral or spiritual qualifications of the believers).

2:12b we-1 (comfort ⟶ you)   vs.   2:14b countrymen
                                                        (suffering ⟶ you)

Paramutheomai is attributing "comfort," especially in connection with death or other tragic events (cf. Arndt and Gingrich *ad loc.*). This encouragement which is not defined further in 2:12 is certainly related to persecutions (mentioned in 2:2 as well as in 2:14 ff. and in 3:2, where it is made explicit that Paul dealt with the problem of persecutions while among the Thessalonians). Thus "comfort" (concerning persecution) is contradictory to "suffering" (from persecution).

2:12e you (worthy life ⟶ God)   vs.   2:15d Jews (pleasure ⟶̸)God)

"Having a life worthy of God" is offering to God a worthy life or again pleasing God (2:12e) rather than "not pleasing God" (2:15d). 2:15d could also be viewed as opposed to 2:4e (the same verb, *areskō*, is found in both verses). Yet, these two expressions of "pleasing attitude toward God" do not belong to the same isotopic space: in 2:4e it belongs to the realm of the motivations for proclaiming the Gospel, while in 2:15d the "non-pleasing" attitude belongs to the realm of the attitudes related to persecution of the believers as it is also in 2:12e (having a life worthy of God despite persecution; cf. 2:12b).

2:13e you (word of   vs.   2:13d you (word of
    God ⟶ you)   men ⟶ you)

This opposition despite its elliptic expression is clearly manifested.

2:13g (2:10f) you   vs.   3:5d Tempter
    (faith ⟶ you)   (temptation ⟶ you)

Even though it is manifested both in 2:13g and 2:10f, the principal transformation has a relatively weak manifestation since it is only expressed in a participial form. Yet the pertinence of this opposition is confirmed by the fact that it is clearly related to another pertinent opposition: 1:9d *vs.* 4:8c. Turning to God (1:9d) corresponds to believing; rejecting God (4:8c) corresponds to the hypothetical acceptance of temptation from the Tempter (3:5d). At this stage of the analysis, we cannot determine the precise relationship between these two oppositions (1:9d *vs.* 4:8c and 2:13g *vs.* 3:5d). Are they duplicating each other? Or do they express distinct steps of a twofold narrative development—turning toward God then having faith and rejecting God after being tempted?

°2:18a we-1 (will to visit   *vs.* Satan (hindrance
   you ⟶ we-1)   of visit ⟶ we-1)

The two Objects belong to the isotopic space "visitation." Satan's hindrance is the opponent which cancels the Helper manifested as "Paul's will." As such the Objects of the above two transformations are contradictory.

°3:2b,c Tim. (strength and   *vs.* °3:3a afflictions
   exhortation ⟶ you)   (agitation ⟶ you)

The Objects are contradictory since the "strength and exhortation" that Timothy was sent to give to the Thessalonians were aimed at avoiding that they be disturbed (agitated) by persecutions. 3:3a can be formulated as proposed (that is, with a positive performance rather than a non-performance) because the negation bears on the Receiver (grammatical subject) and not on the verb itself.

3:3b you (knowledge about   *vs.* 5:3a people (knowledge about
   afflictions ⟶ self)   peace and
                                                            security ⟶ self)

"When people say 'There is peace and serenity'" (5:3a) can be viewed as a reflexive cognitive program since no Receiver is manifested. In other words, we interpret it as "people say to each other" or "people say to people like themselves." When this is recognized the opposition of these two reflexive programs does not present any difficulty (cf. the discussion of 1:9d *vs.* 4:8c). The Objects are clearly contradictory.

4:7a,c God (call to   *vs.* 4:7a,b x (call to
   holiness ⟶ we-2)   impurity ⟶ we-2)

This opposition is expressed quite elliptically in a single sentence. Yet there is no doubt that the author opposes "being called to holiness" with "being called to impurity." The polemical program is purely hypothetical, so much so that its Subject is unspecified. A paradigmatic reading will nevertheless permit us to define it.

Table II summarizes our findings. This list includes all the transformations of the warranting level which, according to our analysis, are pertinent, *i.e.*, those which are opposed in pairs. The study of the symbolic system will provide additional criteria for verifying that this list is valid: the study of the squares may lead us to reexamine some of these oppositions and, eventually, to reject them, or on the contrary, to reexamine the text so as to check whether or not a pair of opposed transformations has been overlooked (cf. Table II).

TABLE II
List of the Pertinent Transformations of the Warranting Level

1:5b we-1 (Gospel → you)	vs.	1:5a we-1 (Gospel ↛ you)
°1:8c you (news about Thessalonians' faith → people everywhere)	vs.	°1:8b we-1 (news about Thessalonians' faith → people in Macedonia and Achaia alone)
1:9b you (welcome → we-1)	vs.	2:2a & b Philippians (mistreatments and insults → we-1)
1:9d you (self → God)	vs.	4:8c anyone (self ↛ God)
1:10a (also 5:4a) you (expectation of Lord's coming → you)	vs.	5:4b you (surprise at Day of the Lord → you)
1:10b God (non-death → Jesus)	vs.	2:15b Jews (death → Jesus)
2:2d God or we-1 (courage → we-1)	vs.	2:16a Jews (hindrance → we-1)
2:2e; 2:4d; 2:9d we-1 (Gospels → you)	vs.	2:3a, b, c we-1 (erroneous, unclean, crafty message → you)
2:4e we-1 (pleasing attitude → God)	vs.	2:4d we-1 (pleasing attitude →man)
2:7b we-1 (gentleness → you)	vs.	2:7a we-1 (authoritative attitude → you)
2:8d we-1 (Gospel and our lives → you)	vs.	2:8c we-1 (Gospel alone → you)
2:10c, d, e we-1 (holiness, righteousness, blamelessness → we-1)	vs.	2:6b,c,d man, you, others (praise → we-1)
2:12b we-1 (comfort → you)	vs.	2:14b countrymen (suffering → you)
2:12c you (worthy life → God)	vs.	2:15d Jews (pleasure ↛ God)
2/13e you (word of God → you)	vs.	2:13d you (word of men → you)
2:13g (also 2:10f) you (faith → you)	vs.	3:5d Tempter (temptation → you)
°2:18a we-1 (will to visit you → we-1)	vs.	°2:18c Satan (hindrance of visit → we-1)
°3:2b, c Timothy (strength and exhortation → you)	vs.	°3:3a afflictions (agitation → you)
3:3b you (knowledge about afflictions → self)	vs.	5:3a people (knowledge about peace and security → self)
4:7a, c God (call to holiness → we-2)	vs.	4:7b x (call to impurity → we-2)

NOTE: The programs preceded by an asterisk (°) belong to the secondary warranting level as tentatively identified above.

(2) *Ordering the Systems of Pertinent Transformations of the Warranting Level*

The system of pertinent transformations needs to be organized so that the programs of its principal axis be in order of a simplified narrative hierarchy. By convention, each program is written above the completed performance (and thus the program) that it presupposes. It is clear that in the case of 1 Thessalonians the order of the system of transformations will be quite different from the surface order of the text. But by losing hold of the surface order we shall apprehend the semantic organization: the semantic system has an order comparable to the system of pertinent transformations. For, indeed, when there is a narrative progression from one program to another, the Subjects of these programs and their qualifications are symbols which are in relation of implications: the one (the Subject of the program presupposed by the other) represents the expended form of a value (a less specific form of a value) while the other (the Subject of the program which presupposes the other) manifests the same value in a "condensed" form (a more specific form of the value).

In the process of ordering the system of pertinent transformations, we have consequently to pay special attention to the narrative progression found on each axis. This also means that, if there is no narrative progression from one program to the next, the two programs have to be viewed as two manifestations of the same symbolic value. A graphic representation of this minimal narrative hierarchy helps to identify these duplications.

Three brief methodological reminders: (1) as minimal representation of a narrative hierarchy, the programs forming the principal axis of the system of pertinent transformations are not necessarily related according to the formula $S1$ $(O1 \longrightarrow S2)$ $\longrightarrow S2$ $(O2 \longrightarrow S2)$: many programs which would be intermediary links in the narrative chain of programs are not pertinent and thus are not represented here; (2) at this stage of analysis we consider the relations among *programs* (including the manifestation of the actantial position of Subject) and no longer merely the relations among transformations (as in the preceding stage of the analysis); (3) in a story, a part of the narrative development is, at times, governed by the polemical axis. In such a case the corresponding part of the system of pertinent transformations must be organized in such a way that the polemical axis reflects the narrative progression (even though it might mean that the corresponding principal programs which were merely attempts to cope with a successful polemical narrative development be arranged in an order different from their chronological order). A reading of 1 Thessalonians shows that the development of the discourse is most of the time on the principal axis. The fragmented nature of the story found in 1 Thessalonians demands that we proceed in two stages: we shall first consider the principal axis by itself; then we shall compare the corresponding polemical axis with the few polemical narrative developments found in our text, in order to make the adjustments which might be necessary so as to respect the internal coherence of these developments.

(a) *The Order of the Principal Axis*

Chronologically, the first principal program is P1:10b God (non death $\longrightarrow$ Jesus). It is this God who has raised Jesus from the dead, whom Paul and his associates strive to please always P2:4e we-1 (pleasing attitude $\longrightarrow$ God). Of course, several intermediary programs of this story are missing (*e.g.*, Paul's conversion, and his calling to be an apostle to the Gentiles), but without any doubt there is a narrative progression from P1:10b to P2:4e. P2:4e is a general statement about Paul's ministry which applies to his ministry prior to his first visit to Thessalonica as well as to his ministry there. (To make it short, we shall write "Paul" to mean "Paul and his associates" in order to avoid the repetition of this cumbersome phrase).

It is to Paul who strives to please him (2:4e) that God gave the courage, P2:2d God (courage $\longrightarrow$ we-1), to proclaim the Gospel in Thessalonica despite the persecutions he suffered in Philippi. Paul's proclamation of the Gospel to the Thessalonians is manifested by several pertinent programs—P1:5b we-1 (Gospel $\longrightarrow$ you) and 2:4c, 2:9d we-1 (Gospel or message $\longrightarrow$ you)—which are, therefore, duplicate manifestations of the same stage of the narrative development.

The narrative progression manifested by these five programs considered so far can be represented as follows:

P2:2e; 2:4c; 2:9d we-1 (Gospel or message $\longrightarrow$ you)
P1:5b we-1 (Gospel $\longrightarrow$ you)
P2:2d God (courage $\longrightarrow$ we-1)
P2:4e we-1 (pleasing attitude $\longrightarrow$ God)
P1:10b God (non death $\longrightarrow$ Jesus)

Note that in the above diagram P1:5b and P2:2e; 2:4c; 2:9d are represented as "parallel programs" so as to make it clear that there is no progression in the narrative development from one to the other.

The next stage of the narrative development is manifested by a series of three programs presupposing that the proclamation of the Gospel is in process and expressing the specific ways in which this proclamation took place: Paul was gentle with the Thessalonians, P2:7b we-1 (gentleness $\longrightarrow$ you); he did not communicate the Gospel alone but also his own life, P2:8d we-1 (Gospel and our lives $\longrightarrow$ you); and he had a conduct which was holy, righteous and blameless, P2:10e,d,c we-1 (holiness, righteousness and blamelessness $\longrightarrow$ we-1). These three programs, despite their differences, represent a single stage of the narrative development: Paul's attribution of holiness, righteousness and blamelessness to himself. Therefore, these three programs must be considered as a triplication despite the differences in their manifestation.

This proclamation of the Gospel brought about the Thessalonians' response which is manifested in a series of programs forming several stages of the narrative development. They welcomed him, P1:9b you (welcome ⟶ we-1), they accepted his message, P2:13e you (word of God ⟶ you) and thus they believed. This latter stage of the development is expressed by two pertinent programs: they turned themselves to God in order to serve him, P1:9d you (self ⟶ God), or they believed, P2:13g (2:10f) you (faith ⟶ you).

At this point of the analysis we cannot determine if these programs must be viewed as duplications or as distinct steps in a narrative development: the study of the polemical axis will allow us to decide this point. If they manifest a narrative development, the questions of their order will need to be addressed (by considering the order of the polemical axis).

It seems that the next stage of the narrative development concerns what happened to the Thessalonians as believers (this will have to be verified by considering the polemical axis). They were called to holiness by God, P4:7a,c God (call to holiness ⟶ you), and then they received instructions (from Paul) concerning eventual persecutions, P3:3b you (knowledge about afflictions ⟶ self), and Paul comforted them, P2:12b we-1 (comfort ⟶ you). As a result of all this narrative development, they had (or at least they were expected to have) a conduct pleasing to God, P2:12e you (worthy life ⟶ God). They are servants of the living and true God (1:10). As a consequence, the Thessalonians are faithfully waiting for the coming of the Lord, P1:10a you (expectation of the Lord's coming ⟶ you), (and thus the day of the Lord shall not surprise them 5:4a). When taking into account 5:4a, we find a progression from P2:12e to P1:10a (5:4a). Yet if we take 1:10a in itself there is no narrative development between the two programs which must then be viewed as "parallel." The study of the symbolic system will allow us to decide which of these two options is valid.

The warranting level includes still other pertinent programs. But they form an interpretative level, i.e., a secondary warranting level (not to be confused with the dialogic interpretative level), which is based on Paul's interpretation (his preoccupation about the Thessalonians) of the situation in which he left them (namely, their faithful conduct as expressed in 2:12e; but would they remain faithful?).

After their separation, Paul first wanted to visit the Thessalonians, P2:18a we-1 (will to visit you ⟶ we-1), then, since he could not, he sent Timothy in order that he might strengthen their faith and exhort them, P3:2b,c Timothy (strength and exhortation ⟶ you).

Then Timothy brought back news about the faithfulness of the Thessalonians, and this news propagates itself throughout Macedonia, Greece, and everywhere, P1:8c you (news about your own faith ⟶ people everywhere), which is to be contrasted not only with 1:8b but also implicitly with Paul's ignorance concerning their faith (*e.g.*, 3:5).

The hierarchical order of the principal programs of the warranting level can be represented as in Table III.

(b) *The Order of the Polemical Axis*

Considering the order of the polemical axis thus established, we must remember that it represents only a *potential* narrative hierarchy, which could be actualized in various ways into full-fledged polemical narratives. Since the polemical axis only manifests a potential narrative,

TABLE III

Hierarchical Order of the Principal Programs of the Warranting Level

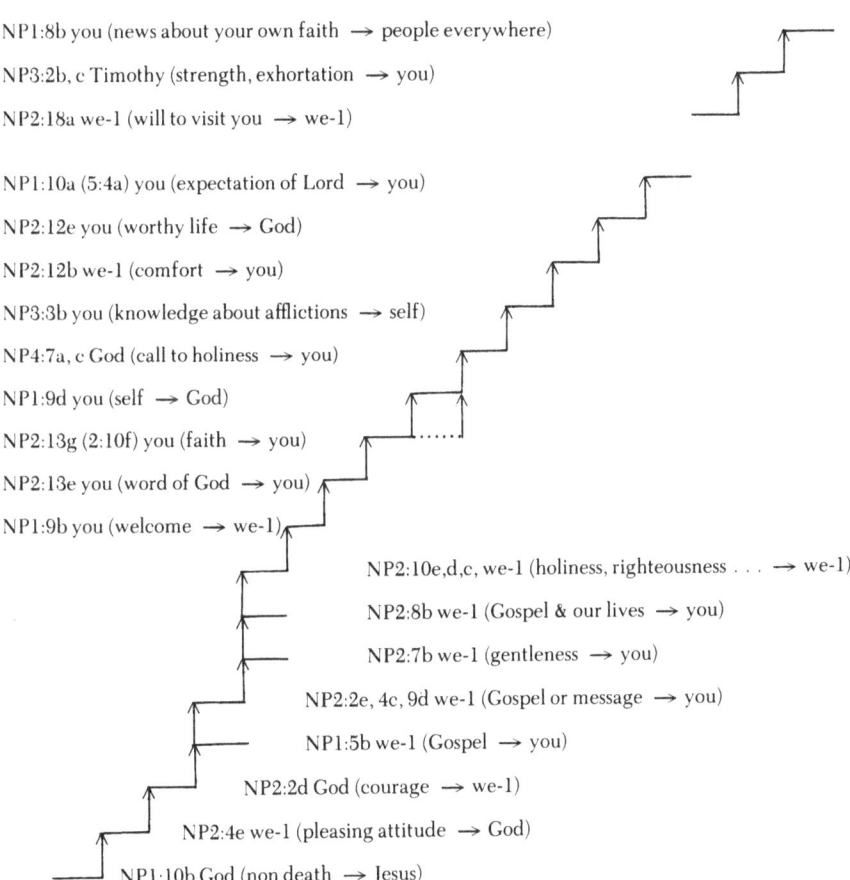

we need to consider the relations among the thematic roles that these programs involve and not the relations among the programs themselves (except in the cases when the polemical axis governs the narrative development). For, indeed, a *potential* narrative development is manifested by means of thematic roles (as discussed above when considering the characteristics of a didactic discourse). Let us keep in mind that thematic roles are narrative programs with a very limited investment of the actantial model. The Object is alone fully defined; the other positions are only defined through their relationship to the Object: the Subject is defined as having the competence to transmit the Object, and the Receiver as lacking, wishing or desiring, the Object. Thus when considering the organization of the polemical axis, we must consider only the thematic roles represented by these programs.

In the warranting level of 1 Thessalonians there is no polemical development which takes away from the principal axis its leading role. Thus as a whole, the order of the system of pertinent transformations should be the one we established by studying the interrelation of the principal programs. Yet a study of the interrelation of the polemical thematic roles provides a means to verify the validity of our argument concerning the organization of the corresponding principal programs. We need to discuss only a few instances concerning the parts of that argument in which the principal hierarchical progression was not clearly manifested in the text. (Consulting Table IV-A will facilitate the reading of the following remarks.)

Let us consider first the relations among P2:2d, P1:5b and P2:2e, 4c, 9d. The corresponding polemical programs are P2:16a, P1:5a and P2:3a,b,c. P2:16a, Jews (hindrance ⟶ we-1), represents the Jews' attempt to prevent Paul from preaching the Gospel to the Gentiles. The thematic role is "hindering the preaching of the Gospel." Now, if the Jews had been successful either the preaching of the Gospel would not have taken place—this is what is represented by P1:5a we-1 (Gospel ⟶̸ you)—or Paul would have had to preach a message to which the Jews would not have objected: this proclamation of a message other than the true Gospel is what is represented by P2:3a,b,c we-1 (erroneous, unclean, crafty message ⟶ you). Therefore, it is clear that P1:5a and P2:3a,b,c are two possible narrative developments following P2:16a. There is no narrative progression from P1:5a to P2:3a,b,c. The same is therefore true of P1:5b and P2:2e, 4c, 9d.

Similarly, the following three polemical programs P2:7a, P2:8c and P2:6b,c,d (corresponding to the principal programs P2:7b, P2:8b and P2:10c,d,e) are three possible consequences of preaching an erroneous, unclean, crafty message. Such a proclamation could be a preliminary step aimed either at establishing one's authority upon the hearers (P2:7a), or at limiting one's involvement with the hearers to a mere oral communication

(P2:8c), or again at being praised by the hearers (P2:6b,c,d). Thus we were correct in considering the three principal programs P2:7b, P2:8b and P2:10c,d,e as a single step in the narrative progression.

We also need to verify the validity of the progression we tentatively identified among P2:13g (2:10f), P1:9d and P4:7a,c. The corresponding polemical programs manifest three thematic roles which constitute a potential narrative progression. Being tempted, P3:5d Tempter (temptation ⟶ you), has for result turning away from God, P4:8c anyone

TABLE IV-A

System of Pertinent Transformations of the Warranting Level

1:8c you (news about Thessalonians' faith ⟶ people everywhere) vs.	1:8b we-1 (news about Thessalonians' faith ⟶ people in Macedonia and Achaia alone)
3:2b, c Timothy (strength and exhortation ⟶ you) vs.	3:3a afflictions (agitation ⟶ you)
2:18a we-1 (will to visit you ⟶ we-1) vs.	2:18c Satan (hindrance of visit ⟶ we-1)

1:10a (5:4a) you (expectation of Lord's coming ⟶ you) vs.	5:4b you (surprise at Day of the Lord ⟶ you)
2:12e you (worthy life ⟶ God) vs.	2:15d Jews (pleasure ⟶̸ God)
2:12b we-1 (comfort ⟶ you) vs.	2:14b countrymen (suffering ⟶ you)
3:3b you (knowledge about afflictions ⟶ self) vs.	5:3a people (knowledge about peace and security ⟶ self)
4:7a, c God (call to holiness ⟶ you) vs.	4:7b x (call to impurity ⟶ you)
1:9d you (self ⟶ God) vs.	4:8c anyone (self ⟶̸ God)
2:13g (2:10f) you (faith ⟶ you) vs.	3:5d Tempter (temptation ⟶ you)
2:13e you (word of God ⟶ you) vs.	2:13d you (word of men ⟶ you)
1:9b you (welcome ⟶ we-1) vs.	2:2a, b Philippians (mistreatments and insults ⟶ we-1)
⎧ 2:10c, d, e we-1 (holiness, righteousness, blamelessness ⟶ we-1) vs.	⎧ 2:6b, c, d man, you, others (praise ⟶ we-1)
⎨ 2:8b we-1 (Gospel & our lives ⟶ you) vs.	⎨ 2:8c we-1 (Gospel alone ⟶ you)
⎩ 2:7b we-1 (gentleness ⟶ you) vs.	⎩ 2:7a we-1 (authoritative attitude ⟶ you)
⎧ 2:2c, 4c, 9d we-1 (Gospel or message ⟶ you) vs.	⎧ 2:3a, b, c we-1 (erroneous, unclean, crafty message ⟶ you)
⎩ 1:5b we-1 (Gospel ⟶ you) vs.	⎩ 1:5a we-1 (Gospel ⟶̸ you)
2:2d God (courage ⟶ we-1) vs.	2:16a Jews (hindrance ⟶ we-1)
2:4e we-1 (pleasing attitude ⟶ God) vs.	2:4d we-1 (pleasing attitude ⟶ men)
1:10b God (non death ⟶ Jesus) vs.	2:15b Jews (death ⟶ Jesus)

(self $\dashrightarrow$ God). This confirms that for Paul the process of the acquisition of faith (on the positive axis) is viewed as first receiving the word of God (P2:13e), having faith, believing (P2:13g), then, as a consequence, turning oneself to God (P1:9d). Then God addresses a call to holiness (P4:7a,c) which corresponds to the call to impurity (P4:7b) to which one is open when one has turned away from God (and turned toward idols). Thus the order we had identified on the principal axis is confirmed by the interrelation of the corresponding polemical thematic roles.

The rest of the organization of the system of pertinent transformations of the warranting level does not present any specific problems. It is enough to represent it in a summary form in Table IV–A.

Table IV–A represents the system of pertinent transformations of the warranting level in a two-dimensional diagram which does not allow us to show how the pertinent transformations of the primary warranting level are related to those of the interpretative warranting level. The following diagram, Table IV–B, shows in a simplified form that the pertinent transformations of the interpretative level are found in a narrative development based upon the interpretation of the Thessalonians' situation after Paul's departure. This interpretation can be expressed by the question: Would the Thessalonians (to whom Paul had addressed the injunction to live lives worthy of God, 2:12e) remain faithful? This diagram shows that the semantic system corresponding to the narrative level involves two isotopies: an isotopy (I) which corresponds to the primary warranting level and a second isotopy (II) which corresponds to the secondary warranting level.

D. IDENTIFICATION OF THE PERTINENT TRANSFORMATIONS OF THE DIALOGIC LEVEL

The identification of the pertinent transformations of the dialogic level is performed through an analysis of the passages we have previously ascribed to this textual level. This analysis is conducted following the procedures we used for the study of the warranting level. Once again we limit our discussion to the presentation of the results of our investigation following the order of the text.

3:7a your faith (comfort $\qquad$ vs. 3:7b we-1 (distress and affliction
$\longrightarrow$ we-1) $\qquad\qquad\qquad\qquad$ $\longrightarrow$ we-1)

Epi pasē te anagkē kai thlipsei hēmōn (3:7b) manifests in a nominal form a transformation expressing an interpretative attitude vis-a-vis the persecution to which Paul is submitted. Both *anagkē* and *thlipsis* must be read here as expression of the emotional effect of calamities, respectively "distress" (Arndt and Gingrich, *anagkē*, 2) and "affliction" ("of distress that is brought about by outward circumstances," Arndt and Gingrich, *thlipsis*, 1. See also 2). As is the case in all the programs expressing emotions, the receiver (Paul) is also the subject (qualified as submitted to persecutions). The object "comfort" of the principal transformation 3:7a is contradictory to "distress" and "affliction."

3:12c you (abundant love ⟶ brother) vs. 4:6a you (wrong ⟶ brother)

The receivers of these two transformations can be represented by "brother" even though this term found in 4:6a is not found in 3:12c. The pronominal form *allēlous* involves the reciprocal attitude between the brethren in the Thessalonians' community. *Hyperbainein*, trespassing, and thus "wronging" (one's brother), 4:6a, can be viewed as the contradictory

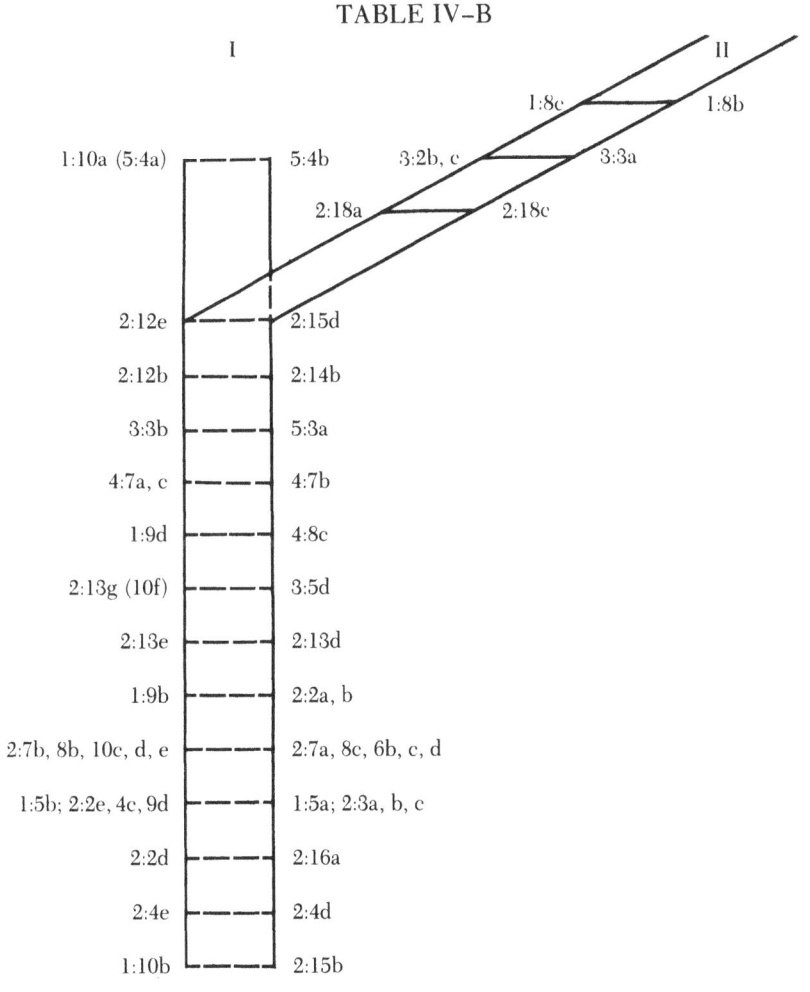

TABLE IV-B

attitude of the reciprocal loving attitude expressed in 3:12c. As is often the case in the dialogic level of a didactic discourse, the polemical programs are expressed in the form of negative injunctions. Yet, as usual, we must make a distinction between the negative injunction itself, 4:6a1 we-1 (negative volition ⟶ you), and the program which should not be performed (4:6a).

4:3a you (sanctification ⟶ you)   *vs.*   4:3b you (immorality ⟶ you)

Ho hagiasmos hymōn is the manifestation of a transformation in a nominal form expressed as the "will of God" for the Thessalonians. Similarly, the negative injunction, expressed by the verb *apechein*, includes the manifestation of the opposed transformation. Living a holy life is opposed to living an immoral life.

4:4b each (thing in holiness   *vs.*   4:5a each of you (thing in
⟶ you)   passion ⟶ you)

Using euphemisms to speak about sexual behavior, Paul opposes two types of sexual behavior that we render approximately by the contradictory objects "thing in holiness" vs. "thing in passion." This opposition can be identified whether *skeuos* is understood as referring to the *membrum virile* (in which case *ktasthai* is interpreted as "gaining control of") or as referring to the woman's body (in which case *ktasthai* is interpreted as "acquiring, procuring for oneself"). The manifestation of 4:5a is elliptic: *to heautou skeuos ktasthai* is presupposed but not repeated.

4:11c you (your own things   *vs.*   4:6b you (what is your brother's
⟶ you)   ⟶ you)

Defrauding your brother, i.e., taking for you what is your brother's (4:6b, *pleonekteō*) is opposed to "minding your own business" or "busying yourself with your own affairs" (4:11c *prassein ta idia*) insofar as the two objects are contradictory as "what is not yours" and "what is yours." Yet the identification of this opposition is tentative because these two Objects also belong to two different isotopic spaces (respectively to a "sexual" and a "business" or "work" isotopic space). We include this opposition in the list of pertinent transformations pending the study of the semantic system which will either confirm or infirm the pertinence of this opposition.

4:11d you (work ⟶ self)   *vs.*   5:14c people (non work ⟶ self)
                            or
4:11b you (quiet life ⟶ self)   *vs.*   5:14c people (disorderly life
                                            ⟶ self)

Working (4:11d) is opposed to being idle expressed in the nominal form (as a thematic role) in 5:14c (*ataktos* is then read in terms of the use of *atakteō* in 2 Thes 3:7, Arndt and Gingrich, *ataktos*, 2).

If *ataktos* is read as meaning "being disorderly, undisciplined"

(Arndt and Gingrich, *ataktos*, 1, 2), then this thematic role is opposed to 4:11b you (disciplined life ⟶ self). *Hēsychaxo* being quiet, involves a disciplined, orderly attitude. Once again, before deciding which of these two oppositions is pertinent, we need to study the symbolic system. Thus at this stage of our analysis, we record both of them in our list of pertinent transformations.

4:13d you (non-grief ⟶ self)   *vs.*   4:13e those without hope (grief ⟶ self)

This opposition stands out clearly despite the elliptical formulation of the second transformation (the verb *lupteō* is not repeated).

4:18b you (hopeful word about   *vs.*   4:13b you (ignorance about the
the dead ⟶ you)   dead ⟶ you)

These two transformations are opposed as two cognitive attitudes *vis-a-vis* "those who died," the one before Paul's teaching, the other after it.

5:6a,c we-2 (non-sleep,   *vs.*   5:6b, 7a others (sleep ⟶ self)
wakefulness ⟶ self)

This opposition is strongly marked in that it is expressed twice in slightly different forms. We represent by "we-2" the complex Subject, "Paul and the Thessalonians."

5:6d, 8a we-2 (soberness ⟶ self)   *vs.*   5:7b people
                                           (drunkenness ⟶ self)

This opposition stands out clearly.

5:9b God (or we-2)   *vs.*   5:9a God (wrath ⟶ we-2)
(salvation ⟶ we-2)

Even though the two phrases are not exactly parallel (it might be better to have as Subject we-2, i.e., Paul and the Thessalonians, in order to account for *peripiēsis*, gaining, obtaining), they manifest two transformations which are clearly opposed.

5:15d you (good ⟶ evil people)   *vs.*   5:15d you (evil ⟶ evil people)

So as to identify this opposition we need to recognize that 5:15d manifests a series of transformations with different Receivers: you (good ⟶ brothers); you (good ⟶ good people) and you (good ⟶evil people). *Eis pantas* refers to both good and evil peopl In so doing, we have merely identified the element of the collective Receiver which set 5:15d in opposition to 5:15b. The validity of this procedure will need to be verified through the study of the semantic system which will confirm or not the pertinence of this opposition.

5:21a you (test ⟶ prophecies)   vs.   5:20a you (contempt
                                              ⟶ prophecies)

The identification of this opposition involves interpreting *panta* as referring to prophecies. Once again the validity of this interpretation will be verified through the study of the semantic system.

5:21b you (good ⟶ you)   vs.   5:22a you (evil ⟶ you)

We take *apechō* as the negative form of *katechō*. Thus we have a positive and negative injunction, in the imperative form, manifesting two opposite transformations: "appropriating what is good" and "appropriating what is evil."

5:23a God (holiness ⟶ you)   vs.   4:3b you (immorality ⟶ you)

This opposition is a duplicate of 4:3a vs 4:3b: in both cases 4:3b is the polemical program. We take note of it so as to record the correlation between 4:3a and 5:23a.

Table V lists the pertinent transformations manifested on the dialogic level of the text.

Unlike the pertinent transformations of the warranting level, which formed a twofold system of transformations which could be established independently from the other dimensions of the text, the organization of the pertinent transformations of the dialogic level needs to be established by considering the relation of these transformations to those of the warranting level.

E. THE SYSTEM OF PERTINENT TRANSFORMATIONS OF 1 THESSALONIANS

There is no need to belabor the fact that the pertinent transformations of the dialogic level do not form a continuous system of transformations which could be construed as the diverging (interpretative) prolongation of a single part of the warranting level. Rather, the dialogic level is composed of a series of discrete textual units. Each of them is the interpretative prolongation of a specific part of the warranting level.

Since each of these prolongations corresponds to an isotopy of the semantic system, it appears clear that, in this didactic text, the primary textual level—i.e., the level which governs the textual development, and that we termed "dialogic" level—is semantically subordinated to the secondary textual level—that we termed warranting level. As suggested in our introductory theoretical remarks, this is one of the characteristics of didactic discourses.

For our analysis this means that, in order to establish the semantic system of 1 Thessalonians, we need to group together the oppositions of the dialogic level in terms of the parts of the warranting level which they presuppose. In so doing we will identify a series of mini-systems of pertinent transformations which correspond—since we are dealing with *didactic* textual elements—to potential narrative developments. We will also show how these mini-systems of pertinent transformations of the dialogic level are interrelated through the intermediary of the system of pertinent transformations of the warranting level, so as to form a single complex system with the latter. We represent this complete system of pertinent transformations of 1 Thessalonians in Table VI. We designate the various mini-systems of transformations of the dialogic level by means of the letters "A," "B," "C," "D," "E," and "F" according to the order of the elements of the warranting level to which they are related. Yet we shall not present them in this order. We shall first discuss the clearest cases.

(1) *The Mini-System of Transformations "F"*

Let us first consider how the oppositions (cf. Table V) 5:6a,c *vs.* 5:6b,7a; 5:6d,8a *vs.* 5:7b; and 5:9b *vs.* 5:9a are related among each other and with those manifested by the warranting level. In chapter 5, vv 1–11, we find on the one hand a statement expressing what the Thessalonians know about the day of the Lord (5:2b–5b) and their waiting for God's son from heaven (expressed both in 1:10a and 5:4a);

TABLE V

List of Pertinent Transformations of the Dialogic Level

3:7a your faith (comfort → we-1)	vs.	3:7b we-1 (distress & affliction → we-1)
3:12c you (abundant love → brother)	vs.	4:6a you (wrong → brother)
4:3a you (sanctification → you)	vs.	4:3b you (immorality → you)
4:4b each of you (thing in holiness → you)	vs.	4:5a each of you (thing in passion → you)
4:11c you (your own thing → you)	vs.	4:6b you (what is your brother's → you)
4:11d you (work → self)	vs.	5:14c people (non work → self)
or [4:11b you (quiet life → self)	vs.	5:14c people (disorderly life → self)]
4:13d you (non grief → self)	vs.	4:13e those without hope (grief → self)
4:18b you (hopeful words about the dead → you)	vs.	4:13b you (ignorance about the dead → you)
5:6a, c we-2 (non sleep, wakefulness → self)	vs.	5:6b, 7a others (sleep → self)
5:6d, 8a we-2 (soberness → self)	vs.	5:7b people (drunkenness → self)
5:9b God, or we-2 (soberness → self)	vs.	5:9a God (wrath → we-2)
5:15d you (good → evil people)	vs.	5:15b you (evil → evil people)
5:21a you (test → prophecies)	vs.	5:20a you (contempt → prophecies)
5:21b you (good → you)	vs.	5:22a you (evil → you)
5:23a God (holiness → you)	vs.	4:3b you (immorality → you)

this is a part of the warranting level as we noted earlier (cf. Table I). The following vv (5:6–11) form a diverging narrative, showing what should be the hermeneutical prolongation of this knowledge and of this waiting attitude, namely "not sleeping" (5:6a), "keeping awake" (5:6c), "being sober" (5:6d and 8a). These transformations form a single stage of the textual development: there is no "narrative" progression from 5:6a to 5:6c and to 5:6d and 8a. Then we find a second stage of this development: receiving salvation from God (5:9b). On the polemical axis sleeping (5:6h, 7a) and drunkenness (7b) would be followed by the wrath of God (5:9a). Thus it appears that the oppositions of pertinent transformations 5:6a,c,d,8a *vs.* 5:6b,7a,b and 5:9b *vs.* 5:9a form the mini-system of pertinent transformations "F," which prolongs the system of pertinent transformations of the primary narrative level beyond its opposition 1:10a (5:4a) *vs.* 5:4b (cf. Table VI for its representation).

(2) *The Mini-System of Transformations "C"*

Let us now consider the interrelations of the following oppositions (cf. Table V):

4:3a *vs.* 4:3b; 4:4b *vs.* 4:5a; 4:11c *vs.* 4:6b; 4:11d *vs.* 5:14c (or 4:11b *vs.* 5:14c); 5:23a *vs.* 4:3b.

In 4:1d,2,6c–8 (textual elements of the warranting level) Paul reminds the Thessalonians of the instructions he gave them earlier about immorality and God's will: God calls them to holiness and not to impurity. These textual elements manifest the opposition 4:7a,c *vs.* 4:7b, which belongs to the system of pertinent transformations of the primary warranting level (cf. Tables IV, A and B). As a consequence (hermeneutical prolongation) the Thessalonians should have now a sanctified life (4:3a), i.e., God should sanctify them wholly (5:23) or more specifically they should have a sanctified sexual life (4:4b). This latter program is a specific instance of the general program of sanctification of one's life. Thus there is no progression from 4:3a (also manifested in 5:23a) to 4:4b. Then, as sanctified people, they should "live quietly" (4:11b), "mind their own affairs" (4:11c) and "work" (4:11d). The phrase "as we charged you" (4:11e) shows that these exhortations were already given by Paul to the Thessalonians during his visit. Yet it is already a didactic prolongation of other teachings (those teachings designated by phrases such as "as you know") and thus they must be considered as parts of the hermeneutical prolongation of the warranting level. This interpretation is confirmed by the fact that the corresponding polemical transformations (living in immorality, 4:3b, in passion, 5a, taking what is your brother's, 4:6b, and not working, 5:14c) are found on the dialogic level.

Thus the oppositions 4:3a, 4:b, 5:23a *vs.* 4:3b, 5a and 4:11b,c,d *vs.* 4:6d, 5:14c form a mini-system of pertinent transformations "C" which prolongs the system of pertinent transformations of the primary narrative level beyond its opposition 4:7a,c vs. 4:7b. (Cf. Table VI).

(3) *The Mini-System of Transformations "A"*

A third interpretative prolongation of elements of the warranting level stands out clearly: the teaching and exhortations concerning the brethren who died (4:13-18), which include the oppositions of pertinent transformations 4:18b vs. 4:13b and 4:13d vs. 4:13e, are based upon an interpretation of Jesus' death and resurrection, mentioned in 4:14b,c as well as in 1:10b. On the basis of a positive evaluation of the death and resurrection of Jesus, the Thessalonians are in a position to comfort each other with hopeful words (similar to those of Paul), 4:18b, so as not to grieve (4:13d). On the polemical axis, ignorance about the dead, 4:13b, brings about grief, 4:13e. Thus the oppositions 4:18b vs. 4:13b and 4:13d vs. 4:13e form the mini-system of pertinent transformations "A," prolonging the opposition 1:10b (4:14b,c) vs. 2:15b of the warranting level.

(4) *The Mini-System of Transformations "E"*

In the three preceding cases the relation with the warranting level is clear because of the proximity on the textual surface of the pertinent oppositions of the warranting and dialogic levels. The three remaining textual units of the dialogic level are not as clearly related to the warranting level.

Let us consider the oppositions 3:7a vs. 3:7b and 3:12c vs. 4:6a (cf. Table V). They are clearly related to the opposition of the secondary warranting level 3:2b,c vs. 3:3a. Therefore, let us consider their relation to the entire system of transformations of the secondary warranting level, 2:18a vs. 2:18c; 3:2b,c vs. 3:3a and 1:8c vs. 1:8b (cf. Tables IV, A and B).

We have noted above that 2:17-3:6 belongs to the secondary warranting level. It is based on Paul's concern for (interpretation of) the Thessalonians as persecuted (2:14). Indeed, he anticipated this situation by warning them about persecutions (3:3b), but also in comforting them (2:12b). Yet he is concerned and wants to visit them (2:18a). He sends Timothy to give them strength and to exhort them (3:2b,c). Timothy brings back good news about their faith (3:6) calming Paul's fear about their faithfulness (3:5). As a consequence of this faithfulness, the news about the Thessalonians' faith was spreading everywhere (1:8c), instead of being known merely in Macedonia and Achaia (1:8b). These textual elements manifest what we termed the system of transformations of the secondary warranting level. In this context, and as an interpretation of Timothy's visit to the Thessalonians (3:2b,c) and of the report about their faith (3:6—even though this mention does not include in itself a pertinent transformation, it does in 1:8c), Paul is comforted (3:7a) and then is in a position to ask that God give them to love abundantly all people, that is also, the brethren (3:12c).

Thus 3:7a vs. 3:7b and 3:12c vs. 4:6a form a mini-system of

transformations "E," which prolongs the system of transformations of the secondary warranting level beyond its opposition 1:8c *vs.* 1:8b.

(5) *The Mini-System of Transformations "D"*

We have just considered the textual development based on Paul's (and Timothy's) interpretation of the persecution suffered by the Thessalonians, or more precisely of their faithfulness in such a situation. Now we find in 5:15 the exhortation not to repay evil for evil, 5:15b, but rather to do good to all, including evil doers, 5:15d. I interpret these "evil doers" to include those who persecute the Thessalonians. In such a case this exhortation suggests, among other things, what the attitude of the Thessalonians should be in a persecution situation. 5:15d *vs.* 5:15b appears then as a mini-system (indeed, a minimal system!) of pertinent transformations "D," prolonging the system of transformations of the primary narrative level beyond its opposition 2:12b *vs.* 2:14b, which deals with the situation of comforted Thessalonians in a situation of persecution (cf. Table VI).

(6) *The Mini-System of Transformations "B"*

At last we can consider the two remaining oppositions of pertinent transformations of the dialogic level 5:21a *vs.* 5:20a and 5:21b *vs.* 5:22a (cf. Table V). They concern testing prophecies and are directly related to the Spirit ("do not quench the spirit" 5:19). Thus the text refers to prophecies, i.e., words of God, and relates these with issues concerning the Spirit. Now we find in 1:5 the statement that the Gospel was addressed to the Thessalonians "not only in word, but also in power and in the Holy Spirit," and that Paul, who proclaimed the Gospel to them, has been "tested" by God (2:4). In view of these relations, the exhortation to "test everything," 5:21a (including testing the prophecies, the new words of God) and to "hold fast to what is good," 5:21b, appears as a didactic prolongation of receiving the Gospel message, 1:5b. In the same way that they finally accepted the Gospel message (2:13d)—a Gospel "tested" by God, 2:4—after welcoming Paul (1:9b) because of his blameless attitude (2:10) and thus, could we say, because they had tested the value of his words, in the same way they should test all the new words of God, the prophecies. Thus 5:21a *vs.* 5:20a and 5:21b *vs.* 5:22a form the mini-system of transformations "B," which prolongs the system of transformations of the narrative level beyond its opposition, 1:5b; 2:2e, 4c,9d *vs.* 1:5a; 2:3a,b,c (cf. Table VI).

F. SYNTACTIC AND SEMANTIC ORGANIZATIONS OF 1 THESSALONIANS AS DIDACTIC DISCOURSE

Table VI represents in summary form the interaction among the various systems of transformations of both the warranting and the dialogic levels. At a glance it shows that the dialogic level is composed of a series of juxtaposed exhortations. At first, in 3:7–13 (mini-system of transformations "E"), Paul shows the effect *upon himself* of his interpretation of the story

TABLE VI

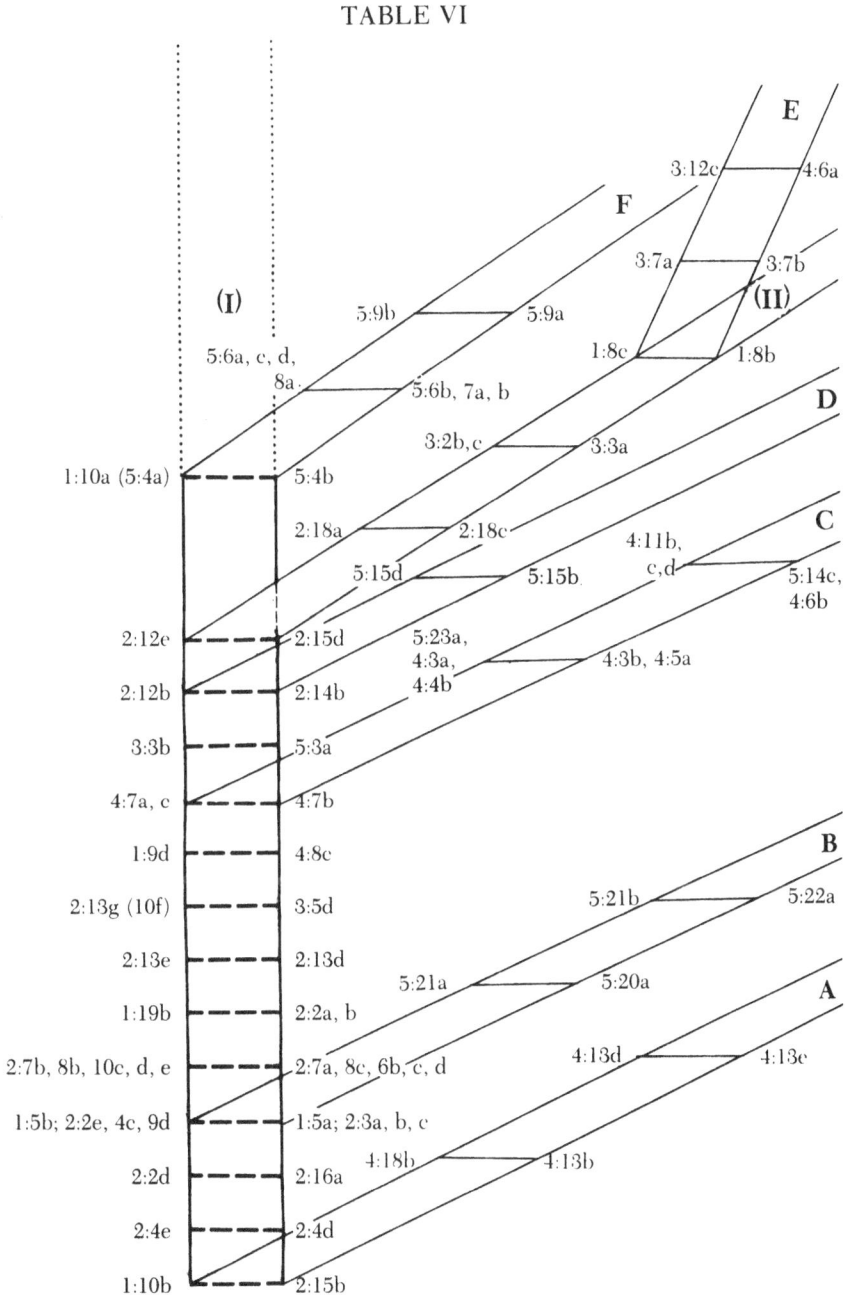

of his interrelation with the Thessalonians: namely, how it transformed his attitude and led him to thankfulness and to prayer that he might teach them further and strengthen them in their faith. This brings about a first, relatively veiled, exhortation to have a perfect, blameless, Christian life: a loving attitude following Paul's example. In other words, just as the exemplary faith of the Thessalonians is the basis for a new attitude for Paul (a thankful, joyous, prayerful attitude), so the exemplary past behavior of Paul toward them should be for the Thessalonians the basis of a new attitude, a perfected, loving attitude. In effect, Paul expresses that their common past story caused him "to do." This is an invitation for the Thessalonians to identify with him and thus to let themselves be motivated "to do" by this story.

In the following sections, the exhortations are more direct and imperative. First, it is the strong exhortation to a life free from immorality which is necessarily part of an honest and loving community existence with the brethren: 4:1-12 (mini-system "C"). This is followed by an exhortation to comfort each other based upon their own faith in the resurrection of Jesus: 4:13-18 (mini-system "A"). Then, successively, are introduced exhortations to watchfulness, 5:1-11 (mini-system "F"); exhortations to render good for evil as well as to help and warn those who have an evil or weak conduct and to do good to those with authority, who are doing good to them, 5:12-15 (mini-system "D"); then, at last, an exhortation to attach oneself to the true gifts of God (the Spirit, prophecies as words of God) and to reject false doctrines, 5:16-22 (mini-system "B").

Each of these exhortations forms a coherent programmed discourse on its own: it spells out the various steps that one needs *to know how to* take in order to carry out each specific behavior. In other each provides the appropriate cognitive competence. Furthermore, together they could form a short treatise/letter on Christian morality which would be coherent in itself. For indeed, even though the exhortations of the dialogic level are merely juxtaposed with each other, they are nevertheless linked together through their themes (as we noted in a number of instances), that is, through specific investments of the discoursive structures. A reading of our text limited to the passages belonging to the dialogic level, and excluding the verses serving as connectors with the warranting level, shows clearly the unity of this level and that, indeed, it commands the overall development of the letter's discoursive development.

Yet, in and of itself, the dialogic level would not be a didactic discourse. It would not be persuasive; it would not cause the enunciatees to do. Here we are referring to the enunciatee, i.e., to the reader as constructed by the text. Whether or not the historical Thessalonians needed to be persuaded is irrelevant here: Paul wrote as if they needed to be. For this purpose it was necessary to introduce under and into the main discourse (the dialogic discourse which commands the overall discoursive development) another discourse which could be its basis. In this way the addressees would eventually be motivated to do, i.e., they would be wanting, desiring, and having to do what is presented by the exhortations. Not all the Kerygma (story of Jesus and the earliest church), not all the story of the interactions of Paul and the Thessalonians is retold. Only the elements which are to be interpretative bases for the exhortations of the dialogic level are introduced. And thus the warranting level is fragmented and partial. Syntactically, and by contrast to the organization found in narratives, it is subordinated to the dialogic level despite the fact that these warranting fragments are gathered together in the first part of the letter.

Yet semantically the dialogic level is subordinated to the warranting levels. The dialogic level is made out of a series of interpretative prolongations of elements of the warranting levels: each dialogic minisystem of transformations presupposes the warranting level, or more precisely, one part of it. In other words, the "modal and semantic existence" of the subject of doing of each exhortation is established through the appropriate elements of the narrative levels. This is confirmed by a detailed study of the symbolism and of the deep values which characterize each symbolic semantic system correlated to each system of pertinent transformations. We cannot present here this semantic analysis: a few general remarks suffice for our present purpose.

Each of the (mini) systems of transformations (on the syntactic plane) corresponds to an isotopy (a coherent set of "values," on the semantic plane). A complete semantic analysis would involve studying the relations of contrariety, of contradictions and of implications among the symbolic units attached to the pertinent transformations so as to elucidate the semantic features which set these units in these relations. But without performing such an analysis one can recognize the kinds of values which characterize, on the one hand, the isotopies of the warranting level and, on the other hand, the isotopies of the dialogic level. In the case of 1 Thessalonians one can indeed recognize that the isotopy of the primary warranting level (corresponding to the system of pertinent transformation "I") involves more fundamental values than the isotopies of the dialogic level. For instance, the semantic system of the primary warranting level involves categories such as the following:

/In Heaven with God/ vs. /under eternal wrath/ as an expression of the category /life vs. death/ (corresponding to the contradiction 1:10a (5:4a) vs. 2:15d: note that the positions of the terms in the symbolic/ semantic system have been shifted as compared with those of the system of transformations represented in Table VI);

/In relation to God and his kingdom/ vs. /in relation to sinful people/ (2:12e vs. 2:14b);

/Chosen by God/ vs. /chosen by humans or by oneself/ (1:9b [2:1] vs. 2:7a,8c,6b,c,d): note that in this way the Thessalonians are established as the chosen people of God while, ironically, the Jews are established as /not chosen by God/ as the contradictory opposition 1:9b (2:1) vs. 2:15b indicates.

Furthermore, the other categories of the isotopy of the primary warranting level can be viewed as specific manifestations of the category /culture/ vs. /nature/: they involve categories establishing the "true" hierarchical organization of society (the faithful community and the interrelation among its members as themselves related to God and his Spirit) by contrast to the natural "evil" organization of society (without proper relation with God).

Similarly, the semantic/symbolic system corresponding to the system of transformations of the secondary warranting level (II) establishes still quite fundamental values—although less fundamental than those of level (I)—with categories such as /faith as relationship with God/ vs. /absence of faith as relationship with Satan, the Tempter/ (1:8c vs. 3:3a) as well as other categories establishing what the proper relationship with God is.

This is to say that the isotopies corresponding to the warranting levels concern the establishment of the semantic existence of the addressees: the establishment of what is the true world, the true culture, the true life, in brief, the true semantic universe.

By contrast, the isotopies corresponding to the dialogic levels involve secondary values expressing the types of attitudes which are demanded or desirable in the context of the semantic universe established at the narrative level. For instance, the semantic/symbolic system corresponding to the system of transformations "F" establishes as pertinent the (modal) values /watchfulness/ and /hope/ by opposition to /false sense of security/ and /the absence of any expectation/ (cf. 5:6a,c,d,8a vs. 5:4b and 5:9b vs. 5:6b,7a,b). Similarly, the semantic/symbolic system corresponding to the system of transformations "E" establishes as pertinent the modal value /loving attitude as altruistic attitude/ vs. /selfish attitude which alienates people from other people and wrongs them/. Similar modal values are found as pertinent in the other dialogic systems of transformations. This is not to say that these modal values are not to be found on the warranting levels, but they are not pertinent, that is, they are not the values which organize the relation between the symbolic units which are the terms of the semiotic square forming the semantic systems of the warranting level. In fact, these modal values are found on the warranting level in the numerous symbolic units which are functioning as connectors of isotopies: they are pertinent as organizing the isotopies of the dialogic level.

Thus the fundamental values are found on the warranting level, which according to the semantic organization, is the primary level as compared with the dialogic level which is interpretative. This is to say that the semantic organization of the text is such that it both causes to do and causes to believe (or better causes to believe in order to cause to do). In this text the manipulation which is involved in causing to believe is relatively limited. As we noted above the enunciator (Paul) expects the enunciatees (the Thessalonians) to identify themselves with him. It is, therefore, more a matter of reinforcing (or legitimating) the beliefs (the semantic existence) that the enunciatees have than a matter of changing the faith of the enunciatees. Such a radical manipulation would involve a much more elaborate discoursive strategy. In fact, the text presupposes that this radical manipulation took place earlier: the Thessalonians have already been converted from their hellenistic religion(s). Furthermore, there is no indication that they need to be "converted" from a false view of the Gospel. While Paul's letter to the Thessalonians is quite representative of a type of didactic discourses, we can expect to find other types of didactic discourses which would involve more radical manipulations. Thus we should not think that the syntactic and semantic structures will be invested in all the didactic discourses exactly in the same way as in 1 Thessalonians. But the general principles concerning the interrelation of the syntactic discoursive levels and of their respective isotopies on the semantic plane that we outlined in the theoretical part of this essay appear to be characteristics of didactic discourses aiming at causing to do.

WORKS CONSULTED

Abrams, M. H.
1953 *The Mirror and the Lamp: Romantic Theory and the Critical Tradition.* New York: W. W. Norton.

Aland, K.
1975 *The Greek New Testament.* 3d ed. NP: United Bible Societies.

Almeida, I.
1976 *L'Opérativité sémantique des récits-paraboles. Sémantique narrative et textuelle. Herméneutique du discours religieux.* Université Catholique de Louvain Dissertation. Louvain.

Bally, C.
1965 *Linguistique générale et linguistique française.* Rev. ed. Berne: Francke.

Benveniste, E.
1966 "Structure des relations de personne dans le verbe," in *Problèmes de linguistique générale*, Vol. 2, Bibliothèque des Idées. Paris: Gallimard.
1970 "L'Appareil formel de l'énonciation." *Langages* 17:14–19.

Best, E.
1972 *A Commentary on the First and Second Epistles to the Thessalonians.* London: Adam & Charles Black.

Blass, F. and R. Debrunner
1961 *A Greek Grammar of the New Testament and Other Early Christian Literature.* Trans. R. Funk. Chicago: University of Chicago Press.

Bovon, F.
1974 "French Structuralism and Biblical Exegesis," pp. 4–20 in *Structural Analysis and Biblical Exegesis: Interpretational Essays.* Trans. Alfred M. Johnson, Jr. Pittsburgh: Pickwick Press.

Brecht, R.
1974 "Deixis in Embedded Structures." *Foundations of Language* 11:490.
1970 *Tense in the Novel: An Investigation of Some of the Potentialities of Linguistic Criticism.* Groningen: Walter-Noordholl.

Brown, R.
1966 *The Gospel According to John*, Vol. 1. New York: Doubleday.

Bultmann, R.
1971 *The Gospel of John.* Trans. G. R. Beasley-Murray et al. Philadelphia: Westminster.

Chatman, S.
1978   *Story and Discourse: Narrative Structure in Fiction and Film.*
                Ithaca, NY: Cornell University Press.

Culley, R. C.
1974   "Structural Analysis: Is It Done With Mirrors?" *Interpretation*
                28:165–81.

Derrida, J.
1963   "Force et signification." *Critique*: 193–94. English Trans. "Force
                and Signification." *Structuralist Review* 1, 2 (Winter, 1978): 13–
                54.
1967   *L'écriture et la différence.* Paris: Seuil. Trans. Alan Bass. *Writing
                and Difference.* Chicago: University of Chicago Press, 1978.
1973   *Speech and Phenomena and Other Essays on Husserl's Theory of
                Signs.* Trans. D. Allison. Evanston: Northwestern University Press.
1974   "White Mythology: Metaphor in the Text of Philosophy." *New
                Literary History* 6:5–74.
1976   *Of Grammatology.* Trans. Gayatri Chakravorty Spivak. Baltimore:
                The Johns Hopkins University Press.

Doty, W. G.
1973   *Letters in Primitive Christianity.* Philadelphia: Fortress Press.

Ducrot, O.
1972   *Dire et ne pas dire: principes de sémantique linguistique, Collection Savoir.* Paris: Hermann.

Ducrot, O. and T. Todorov
1972   "Temps." *Dictionnaire encyclopédique des sciences du langage.*
                Paris: Seuil.

Fabbri, P.
1979   "Champ de manoeuvres didactiques." *Le Bulletin du Groupe de
                Recherches Sémio-Linguistiques* 7.
1966   "Deictic Categories in the Semantics of 'Come.'" *Foundations of
                Language* 2: 219–27.

Frey, J. R.
1946   "The Historical Present in Narrative Literature, Particularly in
                Modern Germanic Fiction." *Journal of English and Germanic
                Philosophy* 45:52.

Funk, Robert W.
1966   *Language, Hermeneutic, and Word of God: The Problem of
                Language in the New Testament and Contemporary Theology.*
                New York: Harper & Row.
1967   "The Apostolic *Parousia*: Form and Significance," pp. 249–68 in
                Christian History and Interpretation: Studies Presented to John

Knox. Ed. W. R. Farmer, C. F. D. Moule, and R. R. Niebuhr. Cambridge: The University Press.

Glucksmann, M.
1974 *Structuralist Analysis in Contemporary Social Thought: A Comparison of the Theories of Claude Lévi-Strauss and Louis Althusser*. London and Boston: Routledge & Kegan Paul.

Greimas, A. J.
1979 "Pour une sémiotique didactique." *Le Bulletin du Groupe de Recherches Sémio-Linguistiques* 7.

Greimas, A. J. and J. Courtes
1979 *Sémiotique: Dictionnaire raisonné du langage* Paris: Seuil.
1982 *Semiotics and Language: An Analytical Dictionary*. Trans. Larry Crist, Daniel Patte, Gary Phillips et al. Bloomington: Indiana University Press.

Hamburger, K.
1973 *The Logic of Literature*. 2d ed. Trans. Marilyn Rose. Bloomington: Indiana University Press.

Hernadi, P.
1976 "Literary Theory: A Compass for Critics." *Critical Inquiry* 3:369–86.

The Interpreters Bible (IB)
1952–57 12 volumes. Nashville and New York: Abingdon Press.

The Interpreters Dictionary of the Bible (IDB)
1962, 1976 5 volumes. Nashville and New York: Abingdon Press.

Iser, W.
1979 "Narrative Strategies as a Means of Communication," in *Interpretation of Narrative*. Ed. Mario Valdes and Owen Miller. Toronto: University of Toronto Press.

Jakobson, R.
1971 "Shifters, Verbal Categories and the Russian Verb," pp. 130–47 in *Selected Writings*, Vol. 2, *Word and Language*. The Hague: Mouton.

The Jerome Bible Commentary (JBC)
1968 2 volumes. Englewood Cliffs, NJ: Prentice-Hall.

Jespersen, O.
1924 *Philosophy of Grammar*. London: George Allen and Unwin, Ltd.

Kaelin, E. F.
1970   *Art and Existence: A Phenomenological Aesthetic.* Lewisburg, PA: Bucknell University Press.

Kristeva, J.
1975   "The Subject in Signifying Practice." *Semiotexte* 1:19–26.

Kummel, W. G.
1975   *Introduction to the New Testament.* Trans. Howard Clark Kee. Nashville: Abingdon Press.

Lane, M., ed.
1970   *Introduction to Structuralism.* New York: Basic Books.

Lévi-Strauss, C.
1955   "The Structural Study of Myth." *Journal of American Folklore* 68:428–44.

Malbon, E. S.
1979   "Mythic Structure and Meaning in Mark: Elements of a Levi-Straussian Analysis." *Semeia* 16:97–132.
1980   "'No Need to Have Any One Write'?: A Structural Exegesis of 1 Thessalonians." *SBL 1980 Seminar Papers*: 301–35. Missoula, MT: Scholars Press for SBL.

Maranda, E. K. and P. Maranda
1971   *Structural Models in Folklore and Transformational Essays.* The Hague and Paris: Mouton.

McKnight, E.
1978   *Meaning in Texts. The Historical Shaping of a Narrative Hermeneutics.* Philadelphia: Fortress Press.

Morris, C.
1964   *Signification and Significance. A Study of the Relation of Sign and Value.* Cambridge: MIT Press.
1967   *The Presence of the World.* New Haven: Yale University Press.
1971   *Rhetoric, Romance, and Technology.* Ithaca, NY: Cornell University Press.
1977   *Interfaces of the Word.* Ithaca, NY: Cornell University Press.
1977   "Maranatha: Death and Life in the Text of the Book." *JAAR* 45:419–49; reprinted from *Interfaces of the Word.*

Patte, D.
1975   "Structural Network in Narrative: The Good Samaritan." *Soundings* 58:221–42.
1976   *What Is Structural Exegesis?* Philadelphia: Fortress Press.

1980	*Aspects of a Semiotics of Didactic Discourse: Analysis of I Thessalonians.* Documents de Travail series, University of Urbino, Italy (Centro Internazionale di Semiotica e di Linguistica).
1980	"One Text: Several Structures." *Genesis 2–3. Kaleidoscopic Structural Readings. Semeia* 18:3–22. Chico, CA: Scholars Press.
1982	"Greimas's Model for the Generative Trajectory of Meaning in Discourses." *American Journal of Semiotics* 1:59–78.
1982	"The Interface of Semiotics and Faith: Greimas's Semiotics Revisited in Light of the Phenomenon of Religion." *Recherches Semiotiques/ Semiotic Inquiry* 2.
1983	*Paul's Faith and the Power of the Gospel: A Structural Introduction to the Pauline Letters.* Philadelphia: Fortress Press.

Patte, D. and A. Patte
  1978   *Structural Exegesis from Theory to Practice. Exegesis of Mark 15 and 16. Hermeneutical Implications.* Philadelphia: Fortress Press.

Peirce, C. S.
  1934   *Collected Writings.* Ed. Charles Hartshorne and Paul Weiss. Cambridge: Harvard University Press.

Pettit, P.
  1975   *The Concept of Structuralism: A Critical Analysis.* Berkeley and Los Angeles: University of California Press.

Phillips, G.
  1977   "Ideology of the Sign," unpublished paper. Nashville, Tennessee.

Polzin, R. M.
  1977   *Biblical Structuralism: Method and Subjectivity in the Study of Ancient Texts.* Philadelphia: Fortress Press; Missoula, MT: Scholars Press.

Propp, V.
  1973   *Morphology of the Folktale.* 2d ed. Ed. Louis A. Wagner. Austin and London: University of Texas Press.

Ricoeur, P.
  1971   "Interpretation Theory," unpublished lectures delivered at the University of Chicago.

Roudiez, S.
  1975   "The Reader as Subject." *Semiotexte* 1:69–80.

Scholes, R.
  1974   *Structuralism in Literature: An Introduction.* New Haven and London: Yale University Press.

Tannehill, R. C.
1975   *The Sword of His Mouth.* Philadelphia: Fortress Press; Missoula, MT: Scholars Press.

Todorov, T.
1971   "Meaning in Literature: A Survey." *Poetics* 1:9–10.

Tutescu, M.
1975   *Précis de sémantique française. Etudes linguistiques,* No. 19. Paris: Klincksieck.

Via, D. O., Jr.
1975   *Kerygma and Comedy in the New Testament: A Structuralist Approach to Hermeneutic.* Philadelphia: Fortress Press.
1976   Editor's Foreword to *What Is Structural Exegesis?* by Daniel Patte. Philadelphia: Fortress Press.

Westermann, C.
1969   *Handbook of the New Testament.* Trans. and ed. Robert H. Boyd. Minneapolis: Augsburg Publishing House.

White, J. L.
1971   "The Structural Analysis of Philemon: A Point of Departure in the Formal Analysis of the Pauline Letter." *SBL 107th Annual Meeting Seminar Papers* 1:1–47.

Wunderlich, D.
1972   "Pragmatique, situation d'énonciation et deixis." *Langage* 26:49.

www.ingramcontent.com/pod-product-compliance
Lightning Source LLC
Chambersburg PA
CBHW032301150426
43195CB00008BA/531